FRAUD CHRONICLES
Part two

FRAUD MASTERS

By

DARREN KEYS

Managed by

THE POPULARITY GROUP

DEDICATION

This book is dedicated to all the loyal readers who were searching for the ultimate series that would keep them on the edge of their seats anticipating the next thrilling page after page. This one's for you. I dedicate this book to my son Darren Keys II for inspiring me to write to show that "there is nothing that we can not do if only we put our minds to

ACKNOWLEDGMENTS

I would like to first acknowledge all of my loyal readers that supported the very first book of the 7-part FRAUD CHRONICLES series WHITE POWDER TO WHITE COLLAR. Next I'd like to acknowledge everyone who patiently waited for the release of part two FRAUD MASTERS. A special thank you to Tari, Kabera, Nikki, Ben, and all of the people who stayed on my back until it was all done; who read and proof read, and gave their time and valued opinions when I needed them. Well here we are ready to shoot the TV Series and the Movie to part one. It's been a long hard road. It's the journey along way that counts so much in the end.

FRAUD MASTERS

PROLOGUE

"Dee, the Russian guy Boris is here."

"Bring him back China. So Steph, your man showed up after all, huh?"

"Better late than never" Steph said taking a sip of Louis XIII Cognac; compliments of the last transaction with the hacker Josh.

"Boris, what's good?" Steph shook hands with the White Russian.

"You remember my friend DeJohn right?"

"Sure, I daunt fur-get any thing. How are you?"

"I'm good. Let's get right down to business. The Russians are supposed to be the best in counter-surveillance in the world, is that right?"

"That's right. So what is the problem?"

Steph intervened, "Do you remember that time the guy was wearing a wire and you knew without ever frisking him or anything?"

"Yeah, Steph says that you can get your hands on a device that can see through clothes and walls and shit."

"That's right. It's called the millivision viewer. It's a device used by the Russian KGB. You can put it in a van and see right into a house, if the walls are not cement. You can see through clothing, revealing whether someone is wearing a wire, carrying guns or stealing from you. It's excellent for security."

"So, how much would it cost me to get my hands on one?" I said with a hint of longing.

CHAPTER 1

DRAMA ALREADY

I quickly dialed Splizzy. He answered on the first ring. "Splizz, this thing is blowing up in our face, this crazy broad is telling me to turn myself in so her and Isha can go home."

"What? Are they saying she can't leave?"

"Yeah, I guess so." Then I remembered Mel was checking on a lawyer. "Splizz, I'll call you back, I'm trying to get a lawyer down there real fast."

"Awight yo, call me back, I'm here."

Without saying another word, I clicked over and dialed Mel. He must have recognized my number because without saying hello he went straight into talking to me.

"Youngster what took you so long to call me back? The lawyer said he got you. He's on his way down there. So you can breathe a little easier now."

"When did you talk to him because I just got off the phone with her and she's scared to death. They're telling her she can't leave L.A. and that they gone take my daughter and shit."

He became instantly upset like he had a personal stake in the outcome and he sort of did. If something happens to me, his business goes back to normal. "Man, I hate them mutha fuckas!"

"Look Mel, I need you to call your man and tell him that I need an update on the situation."

"I'll take care of it youngster."

"Awight, later."

Twyla came back into the room. "Is everyting ok mister Dee? You seem upset, did I do someting wrong?"

"No Twyla, everything is fine, I just got some problems, that's all." Just as I put the phone on the coffee table, the sound of glass shattering and Twyla's scream scared the shit out of me. I turned towards the window and noticed a brick and broken glass on the beige plush carpet. "What da fuck?" I was caught totally off guard. I didn't know anybody in Jamaica and nobody knew me or where I was so maybe it was a mistake. I walked over to the window and pulled the curtain aside. Twyla's scream did not help the situation because the two Jamaicans obviously heard her and began screaming out Jamaican obscenities,

"Yu bloodcot idiot gyal, ya dunno mi nah let yu go, mi ah murder ya bumbaclot firs!" "Yu betta cum now, or mi ah cum fi yu!"

" Mister Dee" Twyla joined me at the window, "Mi sorry, dats the boy, mi tell yu bout. Da boy dere sick inna him head Mister Dee." This kind of shit always happens to me. A piece of pussy always comes with a hidden price to pay.

"Does he have a gun Twyla?" If so, I was definitely unprepared. Damn, I just got here and fucking drama already. All I could think of was the golf clubs in the study room. I might not be a pro golfer but I had busted a few heads in my day and I hit many softballs over the fence, so I could swing that mutha fucking gold club. I grabbed one of the graphite golf clubs from the dusty leather golf bag and started for the door.

That's when my cell phone rang. I stopped and was glad someone called right then because if something happened to me at least they would know who it was and revenge my death.

"Yo Dee, man what the fuck is going on man?"

"I been trying to call you and I ain't get no answer, so I called Rude Boy and sent him to check on you, plus the police is here at the mansion."

"What? What the fuck are you talking about man? My phone was right next to me, it ain't even ring. Plus you know how the signal is on this island." That's when another brick broke more glass. That was it,

I couldn't take it anymore. I had to do something.

"Yo, what was that noise in the background?"

"Splizz, listen, some Jamaican dudes just threw some bricks through my windows."

"What?"

CHAPTER 2

WAAGWAN

"Yo just listen, it's Twyla's ex boyfriend."

"Who the fuck is Twyla?" Splizzy shouted into the phone.

"She's my new house keeper. Yo, I'm going out there. It's only two of them and I got a golf club."

"Yo, you don't know whether they got guns or what. Hold up, let me call Myles, he can call Rude Boy back and see how close he is. Don't go out there yet Dee, let me see what's up with Rude Boy first."

That's the last word I heard before I threw the phone on the couch and it bounced on the floor and Twyla picked it up.

"Let me tell you mutha fuckas something cause yall don't know who the fuck yall fucking with..." before I could get out another word, the skinny pitch black taller one came running at me with a bat. He swung and although I jumped back almost out of the way, while swinging the golf club, the bat caught me on the left arm, right near my funny bone. I felt it go numb; but I was already in motion. The golf club smashed into the side of his head right at his ear. All I saw was crimson red liquid starting to pour out. He screamed like a little bitch. That's when the other shorter, lighter skinned dread started coming after me with a machete.

Twyla screamed, "Stop it Donovan, leave imm alone, okay mi will go wit yu."

The excruciating and debilitating pain in my left arm and the black suburban came at the same time.

Just as the dred swung the machete at me, I blocked it with the golf club but lost my grip from the impact and it fell to the ground, leaving me defenseless.

The next swing of the machete may have been fatal but it was interrupted by the loud gun shot that I also feared was for me, until I heard the voice say, "Drop it or mi ah kill you rite ere inna da sand." God was definitely on my side this day because after I realized that I wasn't hit, I turned towards the black truck and recognized Rude Boy, the Jamaican that Myles introduced me to, who told me that if I ever have any problems to call him. "Dee yu cool mon?"

"Respect, respect Rude Boy, " the assailant said with the look of fear on his face.

"Why Unno cum ere? Waagwan?"

"Rude Boy, mi sorry brethren, mi ah cum fi da gyal dem"

"Who, she yu ah chat bout?" He turned pointing at Twyla. "Yu wan go wit im?"

"No," Twyla answered with the look of fear on her face.

"She nah waan go, seen? So tek ya friend an gwaan, imm look like imm need ah doctor fi stitch up his rasclot. Mi nah waan see yu round ere no more, if mi ere say, yu cum back, DUPPY!"

"Yeh mon, mi neva kno Rude Boy, mi swear mi neva kno." Twyla's ex boyfriend pleaded as he helped his friend to their weather beaten Toyota.

At that time, I felt lightening strike inside my arm, it had to be broken. I let out a loud shriek and grabbed my arm. "Dee, it look like yu need ti go ti da ospital mon." It was crazy how Jamaicans just refuse to pronounce the "h" sound. The "h" is always silent when they speak, that tripped me out.

"Mr.Dee we need ti go inside, me get yu sum ice fi da swelling and then we caan go ti da ospital."

"Rude Boy, do you know these dudes?"

"Dem ah couple punks from Kingston. Mi grew up in Kingston ya kno and mi reputation known mon. It look lyk mi mek it rite on time."

You sure did, what were you........" he cut me off.

"Splizzy called mi an imm seh sumting bout imm can't reach yu pon ya cell. Mi tell imm oww da reception on da island stay."

We all went inside. Twyla fixed us a drink and made an ice pack for my arm to bring down the swelling. Rude Boy promised to hook me up with a gun so I could protect myself, but he also explained that I better not tell nobody I got it because, unlike America, the Jamaican police will kill you just for having a gun. He went on to tell me that if I am ever stopped by police, I'd better shoot first because if they find a gunon me , they will kill me. This foreign country shit is crazy.

CHAPTER 3

WOODLAND HILLS

He and Twyla talked me into going to the hospital, where they took x-rays, gave me some Tylenol #3 with codeine, a sling and released me. During the drive back home, I checked my messages. Splizz was cussing me out, Brishette, Candy, and Rissa had all called also. The lawyer had gotten Rissa released. Brishette had taken Isha to her house and Rissa was having a fit, she had called four times, so I returned Brishette's call first.

"Hey baby, what is going on, I've been trying to reach you so you can tell me what to do about your daughter."

"Where is she?"

"She's in bed sleeping, she's ok, I just got a little worried when I couldn't get you."

"Well, I'm glad you made it back safely and I miss you already." I began to yawn from the codeine in my system.

"You sound tired."

"I am. So, what's your schedule like tomorrow?"

"Just writing most of the day. So I'll probably be at home. Have you talked to Isha's mother?"

"Naw, not yet, but she's called and left message. I wasn't getting a signal for a while, the signal is bad in Jamaica. But I am going to call her as soon as I hang up with you so I can find out what time tomorrow you can meet her so she can pick up Isha.".

"Okay, let me know."

"I'll call you as soon as I talk to Rissa." I started dialing Rissa on my cell phone. The phone began ringing at the house which means only one of three people could be calling. Twyla, China or Splizzy. No one else had this house number on the island.

"Hello, Rissa hold on." I picked up the house phone. "Hello."

"Yo, what's up wit chu? I told you we had a situation..." I cut him off.

"Hold up, I'm goona have to call one of you back. Rissa? I might need to call you back"

"You need to talk to me right mutha fuckin now..."

"Hold up, who da fuck you talking to like that? You done lost your damn mind girl."

"Where is my daughter Dee? And you need to come talk to me. Where you at anyway?"

"Splizz hold on a minute. Okay Rissa check this out, I got a problem on the other end. Isha is fine, she's sleeping right now but I'm gonna bring her to you tomorrow morning. So are you still at the same hotel?"

"Yeah, and I don't have no money to pay them for any more days....." I cut her off.

"Don't worry about money, I got chew. I'll send some money by Isha, but I gotta call you back Rissa, so you alright until tomorrow?"

"No, I ain't alright.."

"What did them people say to you anyway?"

"We'll talk when you come tomorrow. You are bringing Isha in the morning right?"

"See you tomorrow Rissa, or I'll call you back tonight." I hung up.

"Splizz,......" before I could say anything else Splizz told me to hold on and put China on the phone.

"Dee, why you just calling us back? Oh, you called him."

Splizz apparently corrected her in the background.

" I just got back from the hospital."

"Hospital? For what? What's wrong? Are you okay?"

"Yeah, I'm good. My arm is fractured."

"Oh my God, what happened?" China asked with sincere concern.

"I had a lil problem with some Jamaicans, they tried to jump me."

"So what happened? Where are you?"

"It's a long story, I'll tell you about it later. But right now, I need to know what happened."

"Well, I was getting ready to leave. As I walked towards the door, I heard the chimes from the bell and the monitor lit up in the foyer. I saw the police at the gate along with a pointed nosed old White lady......"

"So what happened? What did you do?" I interrupted.

"I did what you taught me to do. Well, I first answered them and let them in. Once inside, the lady started asking me who I was and how did I get in and who's cars were in the driveway? I just told her that we are leasing the property. Well my fiance is leasing...."

"Your fiance huh?" I had to cut her off with that one. "So where did that come from?"

"Don't let it go to your head. So anyway, I went and got the paper work after the police asked me for my I.D. I showed them my drivers license and the lease agreement, then payment receipts, and the ad from the newspaper. The police told the lady that this is a civil matter, just like you said. They asked could they take the paperwork. I told them no. But I called Kareem and he said just make em a copy, so I ran a copy in the fax machine."

"Damn, China you sound like you been through this shit before."

"To be honest, I was scared to death. They could tell too, but the paperwork was all they needed to see. Oh yeah, the lady said we'd be hearing from her lawyers, and they need you to contact them. The police left his card."

"Yeah right, like I'm really gone call them back. I need you to start looking for another property, cause we're ready to go legit anyway....."

"I got an appointment Thursday to see a property in Woodland Hills."

"You know what? I knew I made the right choice when I chose you as my partner."

"Yeah whatever, flattery will get you somewhere some of the time but not everywhere all the time.

Dee, I need to see you so we can discuss this next move. You need to be here if you can."

"We'll talk about that later China. Let me speak to Splizzy and I'll call you back. I luv you hear?"

"Yeah, I luv you too Dee. Hold on, here go Splizz."

"Yo, how has China been acting since that situation?"

"What chu mean? How she been acting? I guess she's been cool, I didn't see no change. She still handling her business, as usual."

"Just keep your eye on her, make sure she's awight, that's my girl yo, I don't want nothing to happen to her, you feel me?"

"Yeah, I got chu, you want me to watch her back. Yo, you ain't even have to tell me that; that goes without saying cause that's why I'm here, for real for real."

"Oh yeah, what's up with the girl Sizzle? What she got you pussy whipped or something? Tell me about her."

"What the fuck are you talking about Dee? You done bumped your fuckin head man, it ain't never gone be like that if I can help it. But she's cool, sexy as a muthafucka, 5ft.2, long hair, she's about a size 6, kind of petite, real petite. Yo, her skin is like bronze, no bullshit, I guess that's how they make them in Brazil..."

"Yo...that's enough, that's just what I thought, she got you wide open. Anytime you're about to go into her whole history, she must have put it on your ass."

"Yeah whatever, you the one be falling all in love and shit. China got yo ass open too....." I cut him off.

"Yo, China is a millionaire in the making. Shiiiit, you gotta love her. You need to be trying to find out how you and Sizzle can get some money together. That's what you need to be doing; because these days it's about a point to point relationship. Both parties gotta bring something to the table and meet in the middle. If it don't make money, it don't make sense. Hold on, that's my other line."

CHAPTER 4

I DON'T WANT TO GO TO JAIL

"Hello."

"Dee, I need to come see you. Where you at?"

"You can't come see me Rissa, cause I ain't around. I'm out of town."

"So why I can't come where you at? And I thought you was bringing Isha tomorrow?"

"Rissa, I thought I just told you I'll call you back."

"Dee I'm scared. I don't wanna be by myself, plus I'm horny as a muthafucka right now....."

"What the fuck you scared of, the boogie man? Hold on Rissa, damn, I forgot I got somebody on the other line."

"Yo Splizz, that's Rissa on the other line talking about she's scared. Let me call you back, plus I don't want her to meet Brishette cause I don't know whether she tryin to set me up or what. So, I need one of the girls to drop Isha off to Rissa after you meet Brishette and get Isha, but we'll talk more when I call you back yo. Awight?"

"Okay, I'm back Rissa. So what are you scared of?"

"I'm in this hotel way out here in California, all by myself. And ain't nobody here to hold me, the poleeece..." she started her sniffling and crying act that I know oh so well. "...Don't want me to leave cause they think I'm withholding information about a murder. Dee, they talking about taking Isha if I go to jail..."

"Let me stop you right there, ain't nobody gone do shit to Isha or you cause you haven't done nothing wrong. And neither have I, so you don't have nothing to worry about. That's their job to try to scare people into telling them what they need to build a case."

"Well, if you ain't do nothing why don't you turn yourself in so you can clear your name?"

"Rissa, you don't understand. You saw enemy of the state with Will Smith right? Well he didn't walk into their trap, he looked for a way to clear his name before they could get him because once they get somebody in their custody, innocent or not, it's impossible to defend yourself. They give you a lawyer that's down with them. People are in jail right now that they know are innocent but they need a body to close a case."

"Dee, I don't want to go to jail and let them take Isha...."

"What did I tell you?" Ain't nobody going to jail and ain't nobody taking Isha so stop saying that. First of all, didn't I tell you I would take care of you? Didn't I get you out of the police station? Plus, didn't the lawyer explain to you that you don't have anything to worry about? So stop worrying Rissa, I got you. Use your head, you're my daughter's mother, I ain't gone let nothing happen to you girl. I still love you and always will."

"You mean that Dee? Or you just saying that so I'll stop worrying?"

"Both, I love you and I want you to stop worrying. You are safe in the hotel, so get some sleep and tomorrow we gonna take care of the hotel and you and Isha can go shopping, awight?"

"Yeah, okay. I love you Dee."

"I love you too Rissa, good night. Get your horny ass in the bed girl and get you some rest, you had a long day. Get some sleep awight?"

"Okay, so am I gonna see you in the morning?"

"We'll see. Good night."

She must think I'm stupid. I did not get this far being stupid. I called Splizzy and told him to get somebody to watch her so I'll know her every move. And I wasn't too worried about the phone being traced to my location because there's no GPS chip in it and the phone is hooked up through a routing service, so they will only see that the call went to a router but they can't see where it went after that. So I'm good on that.

CHAPTER 5

FACE DOWN

" Slowly put your hands on your head and get down on your knees. Now lie face down. I said face down!" They shouted.
"What's this all about officers?" I asked as they rushed me, all pointing guns at my head. All I saw was black jump suits and blue jackets with F.B.I. on them. As I turned to look up, one of them put his knee in my back near my neck as they handcuffed me. That's when I heard a woman's heels and voice that I will never forget say: "You thought this shit was a fucking game didn't you? Mutha fucka, now how does it feel? Huh, mutha fucka? How does it feel to have your heart broken? I hope they electrocute yo ass. I hope your ass suffer, like you made me suffer."
I struggled to look up but could only see the stiletto heels and part of her legs. Then both officers grabbed me by both arms and began to pull me up to my feet and that's when I woke up. Damn, that was a hell of a dream. I sat up on the bed looking out into the moonlit night just outside my window. I needed to think of a master plan.
I needed to quietly get into L.A., do what I needed to do and get out. I laid back down but couldn't get back to sleep. That's when it hit me, shit, why didn't I think of this before. Steph is a movie make-up artist, he could make me look like someone totally different. Damn, if I had

thought of this before I may not have come to Jamaica. I called Steph around 6:45am, the phone rang three time before he answered.

"Hello." He answered in a groggy voice. I could tell I had waken him.

"Steph, it's me Dee."

"I know who it is, but do you know what time it is, it's six in the morning."

"Yeah, I know. Look, I got an idea. You said you knew all about making people up for the movies right?"

"Yeah, that's what I do, but let's talk about this later when I wake up."

"Yeah awight, I'm coming in there so you can hook me up. I'll call you back later to tell you when I'm coming."

I waited til later and called Rude Boy to find out the best way to get into L.A. unnoticed. I called Splizzy and gave him the good news that I was coming into L.A. and for him not to tell China because I want it to be a surprise. I was startled by the deck hand when he came below the Jamaican fish boat called the Sea Monger alerting me that we were almost there. I tried Steph's phone and got no answer. Then I tried Splizzy, who answered on the second ring.

"Hello."

"What's up? Everything alright on that end?"

"Yeah everything is cool. Oh yeah, your girl China did her thing. She got the mansion in Woodland Estates. We went out there yesterday and saw the spot. Man, I never would have believed regular people could live like this. I thought you had to be a celebrity....." I cut him off.

"Yo, we are celebrities. So you mean she got the spot already? Damn that was fast. So what it look like?"

"It's got one of them gates with the initials on it like the joint on the Scarface movie, the front is huge. I feel sorry for the people who gotta cut the grass because it's everywhere."

"Did you go in?"

"Yeah, but I didn't have time to see it all, but what I did see was crazy windows. Yo, the spot got glass everywhere and there is a tree inside the hallway."

"They call that a atrium, I think. So, how many rooms does it have?"

"I don't know. It was a lot. You'll have to ask China, she knows all of that stuff. She just took me and Steph to see it."

"So where is she now?"

"I don't know, when she left this morning, I was asleep.

"Hold on." I clicked over only to find Steph returning my call.

"Dee, I got your message. So where are you?"

"We're approaching Miami Airport."

"Ok, go to the exit hanger. Ask for Chip at Specialty Air Charter. He'll get you to LAX as fast as he can get you on one of the charter flights. I'll be there
when you get there, I'm about 20 minutes away from the airport."

All I knew is that I did not want to take any chances on regular transportation so the fact that I probably smell like stinky fish from that boat beats getting knocked off by the Feds any day.

CHAPTER 6

KILL TWO BIRDS WITH ONE STONE

Steph took me somewhere close by because we weren't riding for long. Once inside we walked down a long hallway to what looked to be a steel door located in the back of the building. He knocked in sporadic code and a huge White guy answered the door with an accent.

"Stephan, how are you? Ivan just got off the phone and he's expecting you."

This Hercules-looking guy just looked at me crazy and didn't speak like I was out of place, so I didn't speak either.

"Where is he?" Steph asked and just then the Russian speaking guy emerged from one of the back rooms.

"Well, hello my friend, finally you came, I've been trying to get you for a week, well four days to be exact."

Steph interrupted, "Okay, Ivan Boris. I'm here, so what is so urgent?"

"You've always been so blunt" the Russian shot back, "Look, I have a Russian friend, Zirelda, who is interested in looking like someone else to throw off the cameras while she is here. I told her that you are the best in the business and that you train celebrities to move right under the noses of those paparazzi bastards."

"So where is she, I may be able to kill two birds with one stone. I can show both my friend Dee and your friend......"

"Zee come out here and meet my friends." the Russian shouted cutting Steph off.

It seemed as if the room stopped as this olive skinned Ms. America pageant-ready sex symbol came into the living room. I couldn't help but stare. She was dressed in a pink sheer cashmere type sweater, which her dark black colored bra showed through, trimmed with fur around the collar and sleeves laced in front. She wore black Gabardine slacks and black Gucci patent leather shoes.

Her jet black, long, silky hair could have been featured in a Pantene shampoo and conditioner commercial, not that she paid us any attention though.

"Zee, this is Stephan and his friend, I didn't get your name." Steph extended his hand.

"I'm Dee" I just nodded as if she didn't faze me.

"How do you doooo?" she said in her strong Russian accent.

Steph pulled his Toshiba laptop from its black leather case and set it on the table and began accessing some computer programs that showed how digital enhancement is performed on the human face. He explained that this was the same program used by plastic surgeons, and law enforcement. He then took digital photos of both Zirelda and myself, then showed each of us on the laptop how digital enhancement would alter looks.

Steph explained how make-up, wigs, oversized clothes, sunglasses and hats were the essentials of temporary disguises but fingerprint alterations and plastic surgery are the more permanent disguises and would cost thousands of dollars.

Steph retrieved a make-up kit from the car but this was no ordinary make-up kit he had what appeared to be everything in there. Steph's many years in the movie industry really paid off. Steph spent almost 45 minutes mixing compounds to get the desired complexion, then he applied this gooey rubber-like stuff to my nose, then he applied some to my cheeks.

"You awight Dee?" Steph asked.

"Yeah I'm good, why you ask me that?"

"Because your eyes are following every stroke I make. I don't care as long as you don't move. Do you feel it tightening on your face?"

"Yeah, it feels funny." I hope he's not making me look like a clown. I thought to myself. "How long does it take to dry? And what you gotta do after this?"

"You keep talking, it's gonna take forever because you need to be completely still until it dries; but it only takes about 15 minutes because the compound is quick dry formula."

Steph handed me the mirror. I could not believe it; he had altered my cheekbones, my nose and my chin. He had me looking like Bob Marley or somebody especially when he pulled out a Dred-lock wig. I put it on my head and topped it off with a raiders baseball cap and some Ray Ban sunglasses.

"Zee, I'm gonna have to get a lighter compound for your face and we'll have to get you some accessories like scarves, sunglasses, hooded sweaters, and over-sized clothing."

"Why don't I go with you Stephan because I don't want her going out until she's almost transparent."

"You can do this yourself Ivan, you don't need me, all you need to know is her sizes so that you can get her the oversized clothing. We could do the obese disguise; I can take her and have her fitted for a fat woman costume, like the one used in Martin Lawrence's movie, Big Momma."

"The oversized clothing would be enough." The Russian beauty protested. I didn't blame her for not wanting to do the fat lady suit because it's probably hot as hell inside of it and who knows who's been in it before you. Anyway, I was satisfied with my disguise, the only thing that kept crossing my mind is how do I explain my disguise to Brishette without telling her everything and she's definitely gonna have questions.

CHAPTER 7

WHY DID YOU MENTION MY NAME

"Dee, what are you thinking about? It seems like you're in another world." Steph said breaking my trance.

"I was gone, I was in my own lil world thinking about everything, you know.....how grateful I am to have this kind of life, to have friends like you in my corner; helping me to get to the next level. Man I appreciate everything Steph, and plus I got Brishette by my side. I just don't know how I'm gonna explain all of this to her without telling her too much."

"Dee, you just need to sit her down and tell her all the stuff that you used to do in your past. Some of the after effects you haven't quite escaped yet and all you can do is ask her to support you, I mean she is your wife now. You know what I mean?"

Steph had a point. "Yeah, you're right Steph. She knew about the drug game before she married me. I told her I left the game alone so she knows how this goes, plus she writes movies so she knows the game."

"Oh yeah? You didn't tell me she write movies. Who does she write movies for?"

"Man I told you that."

"Nah Dee, I would've remembered that. Maybe you thought you told me, but man that's what's happening. Who knows, one day we might shoot a movie together. I always wanted to do my own movie. I've

been around the industry since I was a young kid. My father worked
with Paramount Pictures on the lot. He used to build props for the
sets. So, I always thought about doing a movie."
"So how much does it cost to do your own movie?" I asked.
"It all depends, whether it's a low budget or premium quality movie..."
We were interrupted by the sobering ring of my phone. I noticed it
was Candy's number on my caller ID. "Hello, What's up Candy?"
"Dee, I'm going to the hospital....."
I abruptly interrupted her. "For what Candy? What's wrong?"
"The baby Dee, I think I'm having a miscarriage because I'm bleeding
down there."
"Where you at now? Is Reecee there?"
It seemed like she creamed the word "What?" and the next thing I
heard was a dial tone in my ear. I pressed the redial button to dial the
last incoming call, no answer. I tried again, no answer. Then I dialed
Reecee's number. She answered on the first ring.
"Hello."
"Reecee, where are you at?"
"I'm at your apartment, why?"
"Because I just got off the phone with your sister and she thinks she
was having a miscarriage because she was bleeding, but when I asked
her where was she and were you with her, the next thing I knew the
fuckin phone hung up. I don't know if she hung up intentionally or
what, but the phone went dead. I called back several times and got no
answer."
"Why did you mention my name? I told you we fell out because she
thinks I'm fuckin you."
"Did she say that? Or you just guessing? Something tells me there's
more to it than what you're telling me."
"Dee, I told you my sister is crazy. She might be just trying one of her
desperate little tricks to get some attention. Remember I know her
all too well. I grew up with her and she hasn't changed, not one bit;
still spoiled and evil. I'm just warning you that if she suspects us to
have been sleeping together, I suggest you stay away from her."
This whole thing with Reecee and Candy was a bad idea from the
beginning. It was just too easy. If I didn't hook up with Candy and
Reecee, I wouldn't have met Mel nor would I have gotten locked up

and met Steph. "Reecee, I'll call you back in a little while okay?"
"Dee, stay away from my sister, she's dangerous."
"Dee, where am I taking you? We're coming up on the Culver City
exit." Steph inquired.
"Reecee, I'll call you back."
"Wait Dee, are you here in L.A.? Did I just hear somebody in the
background say Culver City exit?"
(Damn, she done heard Steph, now she knows I'm here).
"Reecee, I'll call you back awight." I said in an irritated tone.
"Dee you need to come to your apartment so we can talk. I need to
tell you something very important that I can't say over the phone and
you definitely need to hear this."
"Awight, I'll call you" I hung up the phone. Steph took the Culver City
exit off the 10.
"So where are we going Steph?"
"We gone stop by my house for a minute." Steph replied.
We pulled up to a beige and white house in the center of a cul-de-sac,
I would never live in a house in a house in a cul-de-sac so I can get
blocked in. The house was small. There were hardwood floors, a
fireplace, not too much furniture, a living room, dining room and two
bedrooms all one floor. This is what they call a flat in California.
"So this is your hide-a-way, Steph?" I asked looking out the window.
"Yeah, you could say that. I come here to get away from L.A. and
think. Nobody knows about this spot. This is my think tank. You
know, the more I look at you, the more you look like Bob Marley with
that disguise, that's damn good. If you can almost fool me, you'll have
no problem getting under the radar. All we need to do is get you a
license in that character."
I laid low at the Culver City spot until I got my new license in the
name Leroy R. Mc.Clintock.

CHAPTER 8

KILLED AN FBI AGENT

Over and over in my mind, I played the scene where I had to face my new wife Brishette and answer a million questions about why I'm disguised and it's nowhere near Halloween. I walked through the door, and there she was as beautiful as ever and pregnant as ever. Damn she was even prettier pregnant. How often does that happen? "Don't panic, it's just me." I said in response to her surprised look. She looked at me like a stranger had a key and just walked in her house.

"Dee, what's that all about, what's going on? Why do you look like that? Why does your face look like that? Plus, this whole dread thing, I so hate guys with dreads Dee."

"Hold up Brishette, let me tell you what's going on. Remember I told you that I owed the guy back in Baltimore? Well, I had to come out here to get what I owed him...."

"You mean drugs?" she removed her hands from her hips and sat down on the couch. "Please tell me what's going on Dee."

"Right, I got the drugs from somebody out here and sent them back to Baltimore, took care of the guy and I'm out of the drug game for good, except there's one problem....."

"And what's that Dee?" Brishette curiously asked.

"Well while I was in San Francisco with you seeing your mom, the guy who I was getting drugs from shot and killed an F.B.I. agent that was his ex-girl's sister, who had betrayed...." Brishette interrupted.

"So what does this have to do with you? Why do you have to hide?"

"I'm not sure, but I think they set this whole thing up from the beginning. It started in Baltimore. The guy sent some drugs through the mail and Fed-Ex delivered the box but nothing was in the box. Anyway, I think they just let the box come so they could allow me to lead them to the source or vice versa. They intercepted the package in L.A. and allowed the package to lead them to me."

"Ouch."

"What's wrong?"

"This baby is kicking the hell out of me."

"But, you're okay though?"

"Yeah, finish telling me what's going on Dee and don't leave out anything."

"The bottom line is the Feds have been asking about me and I don't know whether it's because they think I might know where the guy is or whether they want to arrest me for participating in the drugs being sent in the mail."

Brishette looked extremely sad, "So what could they do to you Dee?"

"Look, this is how I see it, I never sold any drugs, all I did was hook the two guys up. I was just a middle man. So even if I did get locked up, I don't think I'll get much time, maybe a few years because I don't have a real bad criminal record."

"So why don't you call them and find out what's going on and why they are looking for you. But first lets get you a lawyer. I know a few entertainment lawyers, who can recommend a good criminal attorney."

I might already have a lawyer, but until I figure this all out, I got a friend who is a make-up artist for the movie industry to hook me up."

"What friend who works for the movie industry?"

"The same guy who does the home improvement."

"You mean the one who left the message about the mansion and putting in some work?"

"Yeah, that's my man Steph...."

Brishette raised her eyebrows " Stephan Green? A tall guy with bushy eyebrows?"

"Yeah, you know him."

"Yeah, I sure do. It's a small world. He's got quite a reputation. He's been around the industry a long time."

Damn, she act like she know him quite well. I wonder how well they know each other. "So, do you have a personal relationship with him?"

"No, I just met him once at a premier and just heard a lot about his work, that's all."

CHAPTER 9

YOUR SECRET IS OUT PLAYBOY

Later that day I took Brishette's 745i and went to meet Splizz. I picked him up from the strip club.

"Yo, Dee what's up with the costume" Damn, what da fuck! How did you get your face like that? That shit look real as a mutha fucka man; It looks like a professional did that shit."

"Naw, so where we headed?"

"We're going to the mansion, but I gotta make a stop first. I'll be right back." I pulled up in front of the apartment. I left the car running and ran up the steps of my building as it started raining. I dialed Reecee's cell because I didn't want to walk into any surprises.

"Hello."

"Where are you?" I said looking up at my living room and bedroom windows, but saw no movement.

"I'm at the apartment, why?"

"Because I'm outside, are you by yourself?"

"Yeah, hold on let me buzz you in."

I exited the elevator and walked down the hall. The door opened as soon as my footsteps were heard outside the door. Before I could even get in the door good, Reecee was all hugging me and shit like she hadn't seen me in years.

"What's up Dee? What's with the disguise? This is a surprise, ummmmph, and I just got out of the tub from taking me a bubble bath, too."

The apartment smelled of her alluring and seductive fragrance and it did not help that she was wearing a Phat Farm kimono with no bra and she had no reservations about the dark blue silk robe being so loose that one of her breast almost showed completely. I wanted her but I knew I had to cut it off because it was too much for me to handle now that I was married.

"So what were you talking on the phone about? What do you have to tell me that you couldn't say on the phone?"

"First, can you put some lotion on my back for me because I can't reach my back?"

Her kimono fell to the floor exposing her beautiful sculpted caramel body only covered by her black lace thong showcasing her completely plump round ass. I knew if I didn't leave, married or not, I'd be up in her sugar walls until we both came and I couldn't stop there, I'd have to get some of that world famous head of hers too. So, I decided if I'm ever gonna have some control it's gotta start now.

"Reecee, I don't have time right now." As I reached down and picked up her robe and put it around her shoulders. "I got somebody outside waiting for me Reecee."

She, obviously thought I was lying and walked over to the window. "Who is that waiting for you?"

"That's my man Splizz."

She tried to make me jealous enough to fuck her. "I bet he wouldn't hesitate to have me all up in a buck. You act like you too good to fuck me Dee. You wasn't too good to fuck me in my sister's house while she was asleep. You ain't have no problem fucking her and getting her all pregnant and shit, but you always want to cum in my mouth, you nasty mutha fucka. I hate you!"

"Aye Reecee, where is all this shit coming from?" I heard the horn blowing outside; it had to be Splizz because I had been inside at least 15-20 minutes. "He blowin for me, I gotta go."

"Fuck you Dee, all you want to do is use me. I got you hooked up with Mel. I even hooked you up with my cousin Larry to sell your fuckin coke. If it wasn't for me, he would have ran off with your money; plus I'm the one that told my sister to fuck you because you looked like you could fuck, but she saw right through that shit. Yeah, that's right, you mentioned my name and fucked up everything. So your secret is out playboy."

"Reecee, I ain't got time for this shit right now, we'll talk later when I come back." then I turned to walk towards the door.

"Who the fuck you hiding from with that fake ass Rasta look. I still know who the fuck you are. I know everything! Remember that shit mutha fucka." Reecee shot back.

I spinned back around at the door on that last comment. "So what are you threatening me or something? Aye Reecee, you better watch your fucking mouth before you let your mouth get you in a situation you can't get yourself out of." That's when this crazy bitch threw a crystal picture frame at me and it just missed my head as I ducked. It smashed against the wall. I looked down and saw my daughter's picture on the floor and I flipped out. "You bitch!" I charged after her and Reecee ran into the bathroom and quickly locked the door. "Aye Reecee, let me tell you something, if you ever do some shit like that again, I will hurt you, do you fuckin hear me? This is my mutha fuckin house! You better not ever pick up nothing in my house and throw it at me. As a matter of fact, I want you out of my house! Reecee, when I come back, you and your shit better be gone." I could hear the horn repeatedly blowing. I know Splizzy was wondering what's going on. "And if anything is missing or destroyed, I will hunt your ass down and make you wish you were never born." I said through clenched teeth leaning against the door. What really surprised me was her comeback.

"I ain't going nowhere, and you ain't gone do nothing to me while I'm carrying your baby." Reecee shouted through the door.

"Stop fucking lying, you just saying that shit to try to keep me from beating your ass up in here."

"Can you prove I'm not pregnant? Well I can prove I'm pregnant. I'll take another pregnancy test right now." My phone started ringing. "Hello."

"Man, what the fuck you doing? You got me out here almost 25 minutes waiting on you and I don't know what's going on and I don't even know where the fuck you went...."

I shot back. "I'm coming now." I hung up the phone and turned my attention back to Reecee. "Reecee we'll handle this later."

"Dee, I'm sorry okay?" I just kept walking not saying a word.

CHAPTER 10

I DON'T TRUST HER

We arrived at the mansion. There were boxes everywhere. One of the girls had even bought a puppy, and it too was in a little carrying case. There was a moving van outside but I saw no moving men in the truck. I wondered if China would recognize me with this new disguise. Sure enough, China came downstairs with a bunch of clothing on hangers. She gave me this look then shot a look at Splizzy like, who the hell you got up in here.

"China, it's me." I started smiling and she started smiling with a mystery-solved look on her face.

"Oh my God, you are just too much Dee. So where did you find this look?"

"Wherever I found it it's working; because you hardly recognized me."

"Dee, I know that smile and those eyes from anywhere, but I must admit I was a little thrown off. So how are you partner? Here..." she Handed me some clothes, "...help a sista out. So are you hungry? Do

you want a drink or something? How did you get here? Did you fly?"
"Naw and why do you keep asking me loaded questions?
"What do you mean loaded questions?"
"You know what I mean. Every time you ask me that, the answer has
always been yes, I'm hungry for you."
"You probably had your hands and mouth full with Twyla, your lil
Jamaican cutie."
"Well actually I've been practicing celibacy,"
she burst out laughing. "Dee, you are so funny. If you were a dog
you'd be humping people's legs with your horny self."
As we walked up the stairs and two girls I had never met came down
the stairs, China quickly introduced us in passing, "Oh you never met.
Gee-Gee and Monica this is Dee. Dee, Gee-Gee and Monica."
"Nice to meet you ladies."
"Hi," the taller almond skinned one said, "Nice to meet you too." the
shorter dark chocolate skinned one sang as they walked by me on the
stairs.
Just as we reached the top of the stairs and began down the hallway,
my phone rang.
"Excuse me China." I excused myself and answered the call. "Hello?"
"Dee what kind of games are you playing? What happened, I thought
you were bringing Isha, why did you have to send somebody else?
Why couldn't you come yourself? I wanna see you, not your flunkies;
plus, why ain't you answering my calls?"
"Rissa, first of all I never got any calls from you, I've been having
problems with my phone, next, I don't have time to talk to you right
now because I'm getting ready to go into a meeting."
"Your daughter wants to talk to you, hold on somebody's at the door."
"I'll call you back. I gotta go." I hung up before she could get another
word in. I knew she was up to one of her tricks, trying to make me
jealous or keep me on the phone to try to help the Feds get a location
on me, but that won't work either unless they can get through all
those routers. The phone rang again, I did not answer because it was
Rissa's number on my caller I.D.
"So what's going on Dee?" China inquired as she pointed to the bed.
"Would you grab some of those clothes please?" My phone's
distinctive ring continued to ring, annoying both China and myself.

"Aren't you gonna answer your phone?" China said irritated by the constant ringing.

"I'm not trying to hear the nonsense my daughter's mother be talking about, she wants to play games."

"How do you know it's not important?"

"Because I've been knowing her since we were kids and I don't trust her in this situation, plus I need to get another phone cause she might be trying to help the Feds."

"Dee," China moved in closer, "I need you to understand something that's important to me."

"I'm listening, what's up?"

"Dee I care a lot about you and you know that we've had some wild exciting times together but I need to tell you that.......can you please answer that first."

"Hold up. Hello, hello."

"Listen up real carefully because your daughter's life depends on it."

"Who the fuck is this? Where is Rissa at? Put Rissa on the phone." I shouted into the phone.

"Don't worry about Rissa, what you need to be worrying about is your daughter, and if you want to see her alive again, you need to shut the fuck up and listen to what the fuck I'm saying because I'm only gonna say it once. Now do we understand each other partner?" The voice sounded latino.

"Yeah, I understand."

"Okay, you've got 24 hours to come up with 50g's. I will call you back at this number at the same time tomorrow with instructions and oh yeah, if you do anything that I did not tell you to do, like calling the police or trying to play hero, you'll never see your little Isha again. Except in a little box, adios amigo!"

I felt hell open its gates in my stomach. As my world came crashing down around me, all I could think of was why me? I was in shock. China snapped me out of it.

"Dee.....I'm talking to you. What is going on? You're scaring me Dee. What was that about?"

"I gotta go."

"Go where Dee? What's going on?"

"I gotta get some money."

"Money for what Dee? How much money?"

"Fifty Thousand, to get my daughter back alive. They got my daughter China." I felt my eyes water. This was a reminder of how out of control my life had become.

"I don't have that kind of cash in the house but we can get it in the morning."

"Naw, I got some money at the apartment, I just gotta get out of here."

"You're in no shape to drive, I'm gonna drive you."

CHAPTER 11

WHAT'S GOING ON HERE

We arrived at the apartment and as I gout out of the car, China began removing her seat belt and reaching to open the door. "Stay here China, I'll be right back. I'm just gonna run in and run out." I exited the elevator and made my way down the hall, entered the apartment and got completely surprised by what I saw. This was definitely unexpected.

"What's going on here?" They seemed to be just as surprised to see me as I was to see them together.

"Youngster, she called me and told me to come over because she was scared because you threatened her."

"Threatened her? I didn't threaten her. I made her a few promises, but threats......that's not my style." I slightly chuckled.

"So what's going on between you two anyway youngster? Are you sleeping with her?"

"Hold up! I think we got this a little twisted. So let me get this straight, I walk in my house catch you with your shirt out of your pants, looking like you just pulled your pants back up and couldn't get your shirt in in time and my fucking house is smelling like sex and you got the nerve to ask me am I sleeping with her. You gotta be fucking kidding me. Both of you need to get your shit and get the fuck

out my house. That's what you need to do before I lose it up in here."
"Are you threatening me youngster?"
"Hey Mel, listen man, I gotta lot of shit on my plate and at any time I'm
subject to flip the fuck out. So, I'm asking you nicely to get your slut
assed girlfriend and get out of my house before we be fighting in here
and somebody get hurt."
"You know what youngster, that's fucked up that you talking to me
like that, disrespecting me and shit. But you know what? You're
right......."
"Hey Mel, I ain't trying to hear that shit, just get the fuck out of my
house man."
"You know what? This your house, you right, you got that youngster.
Reecee get your shit, let's go.."
"I'm a just get a few things okay Dee?"
"Naw, fuck that! You need to get all your shit and take it with you
because whatever you leave here is going in the trash."
Mel countered, "Reecee just grab whatever you can and let him have
the rest of that shit, I'll buy you some new shit."
"Okay Mel." Reecee stuffed a green trash bag with her stuff and I
escorted them to the door and just as I was about to close the door on
that chapter of my life Mel said, "Oh yeah Dee, you really need to
make better decisions next time."
I knew what he said would later resonate in my mind, but for now, I
did not have time for that, shit the only thing that was on my mind
was getting my daughter and her mother back. I couldn't help but
think, as I counted the money out, who the fuck is behind this
kidnapping shit?
My phone started ringing. "Hello."
"Dee are you okay?"
"Yeah, why you ask me that?"
"Because I'm sitting here in the car with the window half-way down
and this guy and a girl comes out of your building. At first I didn't
think nothing until I heard the guy say, "Dee couldn't have been
thinking when he said what he said because he gotta know by now
that I'm subject to send him and his family back to Baltimore in a box.
Then the girl said something, but I couldn't hear what she said
because they got into a escort and pulled off. "So what's going on

Dee?" What happened up there? Why die he say that and who is he?"
"China I'm coming now. I'll talk to you when I get to the car." I
grabbed the laptop sized Halle Burton silver briefcase from the top
shelf of my closet, packed the money, ten stacks of 5,000 across the
briefcase interior, secured it and hurried out of the apartment.
China had tried to persuade me to spend the night with her at the
new Woodland Estates Mansion as everything would be moved
tonight after midnight by the moving company. I declined because I
needed to take care of something very important.
It was time that I put it all on the table and let Brishette know all that
was going on because it was possible that she could be in danger also.
As I walked through the door of Brishette's house, I notice she had
fallen asleep on the couch, which gave me a few extra minutes to
figure out how I would break the news about this saga.
"Brishette, c-mon baby, wake-up, we need to talk." She looked
peaceful asleep in a fetal position on the couch.
"Dee, I was worried about you. Is everything okay? She managed
through her sexy yawn and stretched as she raised up on the couch.
"Yeah, everything is gonna be...you know what, actually it's not okay.
Brishette, I need to tell yu what's going on." Brishette sat upright on
the brown suede couch. "Is something wrong?"
"They got my daughter, baby..."
"What are you talking about? Who got your daughter Dee?"
"I don't know, all I know is that they want 50 thousand to get her
back...."
"Oh my God, we need to call the police...."
"No, no police. They said if I try anything stupid like calling the police,
they'd send her to me in little pieces, and I can't take that kind of
chance." I could feel my eyes watering. "God know, if anything
happened to Isha, I could never forgive myself."
"Dee, what are we gonna do? Where are we gonna get 50 thousand
dollars cash and where is her mother?"
"I already have the money. I just have to wait for the call tomorrow
and I'm sure when they grabbed Isha, they took Rissa too."
"Ooh baby," Brishette raised to her knees, leaned in and wrapped her
consoling arms around me.
"Who do you think is behind this and what do you mean, you have the

money already? You mean somebody's gonna lend it to you?"
"I already have it in that briefcase." pointing to the silver Halle
Burton. Brishette's facial expression turned curiously cold.
"Dee what are you saying? That you have fifty thousand in that
briefcase?" Dee you're scaring me. Where did this money come from,
I thought you said you were out of the drug business?"
"Look, I told you that it was over and I'd appreciate it if you stop
second guessing me Brishette. I haven't lied to you yet and I don't
plan on starting now. C'mon, let's go get some sleep we will talk
tomorrow when all of this is over but right now I'm exhausted and I
need to get some rest...."
"No, we need to talk right now! I'm not gonna be in a marriage and
sleeping with a man I hardly know nothing about. If this marriage is
gonna work, you need to stop keeping secrets from me Dee! You can
start by telling me where you got all of that money from."
"Listen, I don't sell drugs anymore, okay, so get that out of your head.
Do you remember when we had the conversation about rehabbing
mansions, well that's kind of what I do, only it was a little illegal...."
"Wait a minute Dee, what do you mean, a little illegal, it's either illegal
or it's not!."
"Remember the guy you heard on my answering machine, the one
who asked me was I ready to put in some work, remember that?"
"Yeah, the one you said you work with or something."
"Yeah, well we fix up mansions, but not the kind of fising up you
think. We fixem up to host weekend parties and with the celebrity
guests and fashion shows, we bring in a lot of money. I mean a lot,
like almost half a million dollars per month."
"So what's the catch? Dee, what makes it a little illegal? You still
haven't tole me that part."
"Well, it's not really criminally illegal, it's more civil....."
"I thought you said you were gonna be honest with me?"
"Brishette, I am being honest with you. Look, the owners usually
never know about the parties because most of them are out-of-
towners but if they do ever find out it becomes a civil matter and they
can sue us."
"Wait, they don't know that you guys are doing parties in their
mansions, isn't that like trespassing or burglary?"

"No, like I said the only thing they can do is sue us to get us out and besides that's no longer the case because my partner just closed the deal on our first legit mansion three days ago. So from here on out, I'm all legit, okay? So stop worrying before you stress the baby out."
"Okay, baby, you're right, let's get some sleep. I know you're tired. I know today must have been rough on you. I still have some questions. We can talk more about it later."
Brishette turned over on her side and snuggled in close to me, reached and grabbed my arm putting my head on her round stomach. "You feel that Dee? The baby was kicking, probably telling us to go to sleep." "Yeah baby, I feel it, that's my lil man."
"

CHAPTER 12

GUN IN HER HAND

I must admit it scared the shit out out of me when I woke up and noticed Brishette watching me while I slept. I then noticed the gun in her hand resting against her leg and immediately my mind went "oh shit" and started wondering whether she had killed her old boyfriend and blamed it on her alleged hit-man father or maybe she found out about Candy, Reecee or China or even worse maybe she had something to do with the kidnapping. All I knew is I did not want to go out like this. So I tried to act cool while the woman laying next to me sat propped up against the headboard staring down at me with a gun at her side, as I pretended I was not phased. "Brishette, what's up baby? How long you been up? What time is it? I could have easily looked at my watch. "Baby what's the gun for?"

"It's for you."

"For me?" My eyebrow raised in fearful curiosity.

"Yeah, I thought you might need it." raising the gun, I quickly reached out my hand to help her point the gun away from me.

Brishette what are you doing with a gun?"

"Dee, remember this is L.A., I was a single woman who lived alone. So, I went out and bought me a 9 millimeter glock."

I took possession of the gun. "You know how to shoot this thing too?"

"Of course, my father taught me how to shoot, he also taught me how to swim, how to shoot a cross bow and even karate."

"You are something else. I can see why he loves you so much. Come here." I reached over and kissed her on the tip of her nose and on her forehead.

"I love you Dee."

"I love you too Brishette. I used to think that love was for suckers, but yo changed all of that. Because of you, I believe in love again."

Brishette's eyes started to fill with emotion-driven tears. "Dee, I don't want to lose you, I love you so much and I just want you to be okay. Please be careful today, I need you back here in one piece."

She was so sincere. Her love for me was genuine, unlike the girls in the hood who just wanted me because I got money and oh yeah, the good sex. Love had hardly nothing to do with it, although you'd hear it over and over, it never touched me like this. "Baby, everything is gonna be fine. I'm gonna get Isha back and I'm gonna take both of you with me so we can get away from this L.A. scene."

"Dee, I'm scared...." I cut her off.

"Come here, I embraced Brishette allowing her to cry on my shoulder. "Stop worrying, okay? It's gonna be okay. God is not gonna let anything happen to me. Don't you believe in your prayers working?"

"Yesssssss" wiping her eyes and walking to the bathroom.

My phone began to ring on the nightstand.

"Hello"

"Dee, where are you? My sister said you were in L.A. Why haven't you come to see about me and the baby?"

"Candy, I just got in town last night or yesterday and remember, you never answered your phone, I called your sister asking about you. Did she tell you that?"

"They said I have dilated sever centimeters and they think I'm gonna have the baby today. Dee that's the least you can do is be here when the baby comes or at least show your face so people won't be looking at me like I must have some deadbeat-assed nigga as the father of my child."

"Look, I gotta a lot going on right......" Candy interrupted.

"Don't give me that bullshit, that you're too busy to see aobut your own child. Dee please don't tellme that I'm gonna have to take care of this baby by myself, I asked you a long time ago...."

"Stop right there, I told you I didn't even know you were in the hospital, you never answered your phone. I'mma try to get by there....."

"You gonna try? You ain't try to stick your dick in me. You ain't have no problem doing that, Ouch, Dee, I think I'm going into labor."

"Candy, just breathe. Where is the doctor anyway? As soon as I finish what I am doing. I'm coming awight!"

"Okay Dee, I gotta go these pains are coming too regularly. I love you Dee."

"Yeah, I love you too." As I turned toward the door, Brishette was standing there. I wondered how much of the conversation she heard.

"Dee, who was that on the phone?"

"My son's mother."

"Don't you mean your daughter's mother? How many children do you have Dee?"

"Brishette, we're gonna have to talk about this another time. I gotta get ready to get out of here. I need to pack some things."

CHAPTER 13

WHEN I SPEAK, YOU LISTEN

I received, "the call" in route to Splizzy.

"Hello."

"I must say, you have a beautiful daughter here. She's been asking for her daddy since we last spoke. She really loves her daddy, the question is are you ready to show her how much you love her."

"Listen, we ain't doing nothing until I speak to my daughter and her mother and make sure they're okay."

"Maybe you don't get it or maybe I didn't make myself clear but you're in no position to be making no fucking demands. So this is how it goes, when I speak, you listen, when I give instructions, you follow them and when you're done doing what I tell you, we're through, are we clear?"

"Crystal" I quickly responded.

"Okay. Now that we are on the same page, are you ready to get your daughter back?"

"I got what you asked for, I just want to know that they are alright."

"Alright, Isha say hello to your daddy."

"Daddy are you coming to pick me up?" That's all I got to hear. And the phone was taken from her.

"That's enough. You need to bring the money to the Santa Monica Pier in one hour. Go to the end of the pier and wait. You wii when you see the reflection, you drop the bag into the boat. You got that? And come alone."

"Yeah, I got it." I was approaching the mansion where Splizzy waited so he could follow me to the pier in another car. I dialed Splizzy's cell. "Splizz, I'm outside, you ready?"

"I'm pulling out now."

"So where is China?"

"She;s in the window, she thought you were gonna come in."

"Hold on, that's her now." I clicked over to China, "What up baby girl?"

"Are you okay?"

"Yeah, I just need to get this over with and get my daughter and her mother back and get them away from here that's all."

"Please be careful Dee.."

"I will China, I'll see you when I get back."

"Dee, I love you."

Damn, that caught me off guard, "Yeah, I love you too."

CHAPTER 14

EUPHORIA IS A BITCH

I had a million scenarios running through my head as I walked through the weekend crowded Santa Monica Pier. First I thought about Jay and how he had shot a police officer, F.B.I. at that, and how they would do anything to get their man. Would they really go this far? What if that fine -ass F.B.I. agent was married or dating a psycho F.B.I. agent partner who was working this case with her and decided he would get revenge; a life for a life. Then what? What if this was a setup and the Feds got Rissa and my daughter just to draw me out. The more I thought, the more paranoid I became. I looked around at everyone around me, especially the people who looked at me. But what the fuck, I'm here now. Whatever was gonna happen was gonna happen any minute because I was only feet away from the end of the pier where I was to make the drop into a passing boat.

I wanted to turn around so bad and look behind me, but I didn't want to hint to the kidnappers that I had someone watching my back because they might flip-out and kill my daughter and her mother. I knew Splizzy had my back but he wouldn't be able to stop a frontal attack. The looks I got from people passing by made me feel like Tupac, All Eyes on Me. It was like they were trying to warn me or something. Euphoria is a bitch.

The boat seemed to swerve right next to the pier below and kill its engine just as I was about to approach the end of the pier. Almost like it was timed perfectly to the point of having been rehearsed.

That's when I noticed the flash, almost momentarily blinding me. I dropped the briefcase into the boat, as instructed. The boat took off and two seconds later, my cell phone rang.

I anxiously answered, "Hello"

"Turn around and go back the same way you came. Keep going until you come to a water balloon game, then take a right and you'll see the cotton candy stand. You'll find your daughter there....."

"What about my daughter's mother?" I swiftly asked hoping that she also was being released somewhere simultaneously, but there was no response only a dial tone. I did not like the way this was turning out. Maybe it was the Feds keeping Rissa to testify against me, but that can't be because they would have arrested me. All I could say is that this shit really is crazy. I guess that shit Biggie said is real, "More money, more problems."

As I walked through the Amusement park atmosphere to the water balloon game, I spotted Splizzy and the look on his face was not what I expected. He didn't seem afraid or desperate like I was, maybe because it wasn't his daughter and baby's mother, but still the look wasn't there.

A feeling of relief came over me when I turned and saw my daughter at the cotton candy stand. She ran to me.

"Daddy, Daddy!" I never appreciated being a father more than that moment. Seeing her face light up just knowing that she could have been killed.

"Are you okay baby?" I hugged her as tight as I could, "Did they hurt you?"

"No daddy, they said they were friends of yours, but they wouldn't let me see mommy. Did mommy do something bad daddy?"

"Why you ask that Isha?"

"That man said mommy did something real bad and she was in trouble. What did mommy do daddy? Is mommy in jail daddy?"

"I don't know yet baby, but don't worry we'll find out. Come on let's get you home."

I tried to call the number back to the kidnappers, but got no answer. I started wondering whether I'd get another call wanting another ransom for Rissa. I'd just have to wait for the call. I didn't want my daughter worrying, but I had no clue where her mother was. Splizzy reached for Isha, "Hey Ish. How's my goddaughter? Are you okay?" He said in a fatherly tone. "Yesssss."

"Let's get out of here." I stated, looking around at everybody around me. Looking to see if anybody as much as looked at me funny. I had revenge running through my veins. This was unfair because I didn't even know who my revenge should be directed at. The ringing of my cell offered me a momentary escape from the prison of revenge that permeated my mind and body. "Hello."

"Dee, where are you? I thought you said you were coming. The doctor said I'm going to have the baby today. I need you her Dee."

"Candy, listen I'm trying to get there as fast as I can. I gotta take my daughter home. As soon as I make sure she's okay, I'll be right there. Awright?"

"Oooh, oh shit. Dee the contractions are real close. This baby is ready and so am I. Please don't leave me by myself to have this baby."

"Candy, hold on." I clicked over to the other line. "Hello."

"Dee, are you okay? Did you get your daughter back?" China anxiously inquired.

"Yeah, China. I'm on my way to you right now. I'm bringing Isha to you cause I got to make a run real fast and take care of something, but I gotta call you back because I got somebody on the other line."

"Okay." I clicked back over to Candy cursing me out.

"Why the fuck you had me holding on all that time Dee? I'm laying here getting ready to have your baby, what can be more important?"

"Candy, Candy!" I shouted, "Cut it out! I got to make arrangements for my daughter because I'm not bringing her with me."

"Please hurry up Dee....owwwwwww, this shit hurts. I'll be glad when this all over. I want this baby to hurry up and come." She sounded like she was in super pain and all that tough talk went right out the window when those pains struck her ass.

"Candy, I'm on my way awright. I gotta go."

"Why?" She whined into the phone. "Why you gotta go?"

"Candy, don't start that. I just told you what's up. I'll call you back, okay?"

We were now pulling up outside the new mansion. I had Splizzy take

Isha inside and instructed him to
book a flight for the three of us. Then I called Brishette to see if she
was ready.

"Brishette, are you ready?"

"Yes, I was waiting for you. Is everything okay?"

"Yeah, I got Isha, but not her mother."

"So, where is her mother? Did they say anything about when you'd
get her back?" although Brishh seemed genuinely concerned, I really
didn't want to talk about it to her because it made me think of how
truly powerless I am in this situation and that made me frustrated. I
answered in a way that she would get the message. "I don't know.
We'll talk about that when I get there. I'll be there as soon as I get
finished what I have to do. I'm gonna make a stop real fast and then
I'll pick you up, okay? I'll call back when I'm on my way."

"Be careful Dee, I love you." Brishette had a calming effect on me.
Just the way she mesmerized me with her alluring French accented
voice saying, "I love you," was soothing enough to calm some of my
storm that seemed like a shadow because it seemed to follow me.
Damn, I know the old saying that says, "What don't kill you, will only
make me stronger," but sometimes even though it didn't kill you, it
sure as hell made you wish you were dead.

CHAPTER 15

FBI YOU'RE UNDER ARREST

I dialed 411 on my cell phone and had the operator connect me to the hospital's information line. They walked me through from my location to the mega structure and its busy parking lot, which reminded me of an airport parking lot because it was so busy. Once inside, I explained to the security guard that I was expecting a baby any moment and gave him Candy's name and was directed to the2nd floor. The corridors were huge. The smell of sterilization and disinfectant filled the cool hospital air.

There was something wrong; I could feel it. I thought it may have been just the anxiety of knowing Candy was getting ready to have a baby. This, I eventually have to explain to my wife how I got another woman pregnant while we were together or maybe even the thought of walking in the delivery room and she's already had the baby and she didn't make it, leaving me a single parent. I continued down the hall until I reached the nurse's station, who directed me to the delivery room. As I walked through the double doors, thee she was lying on the delivery table with her feet snug in what looked like clamps, so that her legs were propped up in a push-easy position. She was covered with a blue sterile operating blanket.

I walked to her side and grabbed her hand to offer my support, that's when one of the doctors in green scrubs told me that I must put on scrubs. The nurse then handed me the scrubs. That's when Candy squeezed the shit out of my hand. Our eyes met and while I thought that she may have squeezed my hand out of pain, there was something different in her eyes. It wasn't pain, it was more a look of fear or warning because she kept cutting her eyes towards the doctors. That's when the doctor wearing the lab coat asked me, "Sir, are you the father?"

"Yes." I thought he was about to tell me that the baby wasn't going to make it or something, but he asked me for I.D. That was strange but it didn't hit me until I saw two men outside the door. At the same time I saw the men, Candy screamed out, "Dee, they are the police, run baby," but it was too late.

The one in the lab coat yelled out, "FBI you're under arrest." I wanted to run from the grip he had on my arm, but the two men burst through the doors screaming, "Let me see your hands." I couldn't believe this shit. All I could think about was my daughter and was her mother in on this.

As they handcuffed me, I asked, "What is this all about? What am I being arrested for?"

"You don't know?" one of them sarcastically shot back, "How about conspiracy to distribute drugs and who knows, you may be charged with murdering an FBI agent, if you're lucky. You might want to think about helping yourself because if not, you're going away for a long time."

As we walked down the hall toward the elevator, I spotted Reecee. She had her hair in a ponytail, wearing tight fitting jeans and a white blouse. She had an evil sinister grin on her face. Her words rang out in my head, "How do you feel now playboy? That shit ain't funny now, is it? This is what happens when you treat me like shit motherfucker, I bet you won't be treating me like shit no more. I hope they keep you in there forever. I stayed so you could see that it was me who set your ass up, not my sister.

I tried to break away from the FBI to get at Reecee, but they managed to constrain me. That bitch set me up after all I did for her. "Fuck you Reecee!" The elevator silenced her tormenting voice as the doors closed.

CHAPTER 16

THEY FOUND HER BODY

It was too late to see the Federal judge for a bond, so I was detained in downtown L.A. at the new Federal building for a unsuccessful debriefing before being taken to the L.A. County Jail for processing. I was interviewed by counselors who asked me was there any reason that I couldn't be placed in general population, then the doctors who asked was I suicidal---like they really give a fuck.

They finished processing me around 8:45p.m., gave me a bed-roll and sent me upstairs. It wasn't as bad as the State. It had several T.V.'s, one for the news, one for B.E.T. of course, one of the movies, and even had one for Spanish inmates. I couldn't make a call because my PAC number, the number they give you to access the phone, was not working yet. I went to bed hungry as hell. My cellie was an older Indian guy with long hair. We talked for a while until we fell asleep because between him snoring and me thinking about how many different things that I should have done and how when I felt something was wrong, I should have turned and walked away.

I went to bed so hungry that my stomach growled its way to sleep. At 9:00a.m. I appeared before a Federal Magistrate Judge who obviously pre-appointed the Federal Public Defender's Office to represent me. I was denied bond because there was an on-going murder investigation and the Public Defender informed me that I supposedly conspired with people known and unknown to the Grand

Jury. What the hell did that mean?

After being transported back to the jail, I called Brishette and told her what was going on. I could feel her pain through the phone. I then called China, Aisha, and Splizzy, explaining to Splizzy and China that I needed a really good lawyer, who can get me out of this crazy shit because they really don't have anything on me, unless they are hiding something.

The visiting schedule was done by the last two digits of your inmate number. Mine was 63, so my visiting days were Thursdays and Saturdays. Thursday didn't come soon enough. I had paid two packs of jailhouse duplex cookies for a haircut and to make a crease in my green prison uniform. I carefully placed them under the 12 feet vinyl covered mat. Took me a shower just after the afternoon count, so that I would be prepared to visit with my daughter, China and Splizzy. Splizzy stated he had something very important to tell me that couldn't be discussed over the phone. Sure enough, at 5:28p.m., the pod officer called over the speaker, "Patterson, you have a visit."

I had spoken to Splizzy 45 minutes earlier and they were on their way, so I was ready. I was escorted to the visiting area where they awaited anxiously. My daughter began crying when she saw me, which caused me to want to get out of there even more so I could get out there and take care of my daughter, especially not knowing what was going on with her mother.

In fact, that's the first question I asked after greeting them. "So have Rissa called?"

"No, but we'll talk about that because that's one of the things I came to talk to you about." Splizz said with a poker face. He knew something that I didn't. "China and Isha are leaving and going out to the care a little early so that we can talk, so enjoy your visit and we'll talk later."

I didn't know whether he had something to tell me about China, maybe she was seeing somebody or even worst, like holding out on money made from the mansion parties. Maybe he had heard something about the Feds finding out about the murder. Whatever it was, it could wait until I finished visiting with Isha and China. They were both looking gorgeous.

"Look at you Isha, you look so pretty. Who did your hair?" I asked while touching her ponytail.

"Daddy Miss China's house is so big. You could get lost in there and we gotta talk on the intercom system because it's so big Daddy!"

"Is that right? So you two have been having a ball, huh?" I asked as I tickled Isha causing her to giggle and squirm to get away.

"Your daughter is a mess and she got expensive taste to be a little girl," China stated. "But she's good company though, ain't that right Isha?" China was 'not wearing' but she was 'showcasing' the fitting black two-piece Donna Karan pant suit that I had bought her from Nordstrom Couture Department. Damn, she looked good. Her pure black silky hair was pulled back into a ponytail also, which really showed off her chinky eyes and slightly high forehead and cheekbones.

"Daddy, what did you do to get in here? Is it the same kind of trouble that man said mommy was in?"

She didn't mean any harm, but that really hit a nerve. All eyes were on me. Splizz and China gave me a look as if to hint that they too were waiting for an answer to Isha's question. The truth was, I didn't know how to answer her question.

"Isha, I don't know what kind of trouble your mother is in. I hope she's not in any trouble at all. If she is, I'm sure she'll be calling to let us know. Okay baby? Oh yeah, I need somebody to get my phone out of my property. I'll do a release form. Rissa might be trying to call."

"We don't have the number." China answered.

"Yo Dee, I heard something but now is not the right time. As a matter of fact, ahh.........hey Isha? Are you hungry? You want something to drink? China why don't you take Isha to get something to eat from the machines."

China caught the hint. "Come on Isha, let's get something good to eat." China took Isha to the machines, giving Splizzy and I the opportunity to talk without them having to leave early. I didn't like that idea anyway.

"So what's going on Splizz? You got this look on your face and you know I know that look. Remember, I know your ass. So what you gotta tell me? The look on his face was not good. "Dee, you're not gonna like what I'm about to tell you. It's bad. No, it's real bad...."

I cut him off. "Look, save me all the drama and just get it out." I said becoming frustrated.

"Dee, Rissa is dead! They found her body the day before yesterday."

"What? What the fuck are you talking about Splizz? Rissa ain't dead. It must be somebody that looks like her or something." I was starting to get that feeling in my stomach. The feeling of anxiety overtook me suddenly. My mind was saying that it couldn't be, but my body felt that it was true.

"Splizzy, where did you get this information from?"

"Dee, it was on the news. They said she was a witness in a murder investigation and they believe that whoever murdered the Baltimore police officer, also may have killed Rissa. Dee, I'm really sorry man."

"Isha thinks her mother is in jail. How the fuck am I gonna tell her that her mother is dead?"

"It wouldn't surprise me if the feds come to talk to you. They might have you as a suspect, just to see if you know anything. Don't even talk to them without a lawyer present because they're famous for saying you said some shit you never said."

"So what's up with the lawyer? You find one yet?" Isha and China came back with barbeque chicken wings, fish sandwiches, and the sprite remixes.

Splizzy wrapped it up by saying China had talked to a lawyer. "China tell Dee about the lawyer you spoke to."

All I could think about was my daughter and how not having a mother would affect her. I hugged her tightly as she sat down in the chair next to me. I didn't know how to tell a little girl that loved her mother so much, that her mother is dead and that her daddy is in jail, with no bond and might get some time.

"China, have you talked to Steph?"

"Yeah, he called last night. He said he got you. He's getting you the best lawyer money can buy. Johnny Cochran if he can get him. He said he'll be to see you and gonna try to get you in front of another judge to see if we can get you a bond."

"Okay, lets wrap it up. Visiting is over," shouted one of the nasty tobacco chewing officers. I decided I would wait to tell Isha about her mother, that would give me a chance to confirm it and I didn't want her to walk out after telling her about her mother's untimely death.

CHAPTER 17

10 MINUTE RECESS

I didn't see them again until my next court appearance where they witnessed me getting denied bond again even after my lawyer argued, "judge my client daughter's mother was recently murdered and my client needs to make funeral arrangements, apart of which is to get her body back to Maryland your honor."
"Well isn't there other family members who can take care of this?" The court responded.
"Your honor, with all due respect, his daughter is here today, who was brought from L.A. by her mother to see her father, and they have no family here your honor."
By the time my daughter heard all of this she began screaming. It got crazy after that. I got up, Isha started running towards the defense table from the seats three rows behind us. Next thing I knew she was hugging me, sharing the pain of her mother's death. The Marshall moved to stop me, while the others in the back ran to the isle to get Isha, to go back to her seat. "Your honor can I please have a minute with my daughter? You can see that she needs me right now. Please your honor."
The judge passed the buck and said "That's up to the Marshalls, so you'll have to ask them. But it won't be right now because we are not done here. So you both need to take your seats."
Damn, these people are cruel, but I didn't want to blow my chance of getting a bond so I told Splizzy to get Isha. I knew if he didn't, I might

snap on the Marshalls if he put his hands on my daughter. I couldn't even console her. Then I couldn't blame the lawyer for saying it out loud, because he was trying to help me get bond.

"We are going to take a short 10 minute recess and I'll make my decision when I return."

The Marshalls allowed me to talk to my daughter for a couple of minutes, from the first row but wouldn't let her come up front with me anymore. The reason they gave was security.

As I sat at the defense table turned half-way around talking to my daughter, I noticed the cherry oak wood double doors swing open and my heart started beating faster than normal, sort of like an anxiety attach when I saw Brishette walk into the court room followed by Steph and Mel behind them of all people. I didn't know whether to be upset, surprised, grateful or what. I chose the latter. I got a surge of confidence when I found out my whole supporting team was in the court room.

I also began wondering about the drama that may become of China and Brishette meeting and there was now way I could control the meeting while I was locked .

"All rise." Dutifully announced the bailiff.

I whispered to my attorney. "My wife is here. She's in the back."

"Oh yeah?" he asked turning to look over his shoulder, "Which one? Judge, I'd like to inform the court that Mr. Patterson's wife is here and Judge as I understand it, Mrs. Patterson is here to offer her surety that Mr. Patterson will appear for any and all court appearances. Might I point out that Mrs. Patterson is a well known Hollywood screen writer."

The judge wore a puzzled look on his face. "Okay, let me get this straight, Mr. Patterson is a widow who has re-married already?"

I couldn't let him get away with that one, "Your honor, may I speak?"

"You certainly may because I'm interested in what you have to say for yourself."

"Your honor, let me help you out here. I'm originally from Maryland and I have a daughter with the deceased. We had split up years ago, but now I'm married to Brishette, a native of Los Angeles and we live here now." If looks could kill, I would've died from the look China gave me. She wore a look of surprise and disgust.

"Mr. Patterson, you may resume your seat. Let me hear from Mrs. Patterson then we'll have the government weigh in. Mrs. Patterson, why don't you come on up here."

Brishette wobbled up to the front of the court. She was so beautiful, her long black silky hair down her back. She still captured the audience even with her bloated stomach and slightly enlarged breast. She wore a pink smock-like dress over a pair of black maternity pants.

"I'm being asked to consider allowing bond until trial. Alright Ms. Patterson, how can you assure me that Mr. Patterson will not be out this door and we never see him again?"

Everyone focused their attention on Brishette as she approached the podium. It was just something about her that changed the whole scene of things.

The judge asked, "So Mrs. Patterson, what is your full name and occupation, then tell this court how you can make a difference in assuring that Mr. Patterson will appear for his court appearance if I release him today.."

"My name is Brishette Patterson, I'm a professional screen-writer for Paramount and Sony Pictures. Your honor I will pledge all that I have, my properties and my inheritance, because all that I have means nothing to me without my husband. Also, your honor as you can see, I'm about to have our first child, and I need him home your honor...."

My attorney interrupted, "Your honor, may I also ask that the court consider that the U.S. Attorney was initially considering conspiracy drug charges but the alleged co-conspirator has never been arrested, therefore my client is being charged separately with attempt to distribute. Your honor, no drugs were ever found at all and my client's looking at no more than 36 to 48 months and it would appear that section 2X1.1 would apply in this case for attempt. That would reduce the offense level by three your Honor, drastically reducing the sentence even further. One other thing, I'd like to bring to the court's attention, is that the government has been investigating a murder of an FBI Agent and has found that my client, Mr. Patterson, had no involvement and therefore has been cleared of all charges, as it relates to that case. So what we actually have here your Honor is simply an attempt to distribute."

"Your Honor, Mr. Patterson was wearing a disguise when he was apprehended at the hospital, where he showed up to see another of his children being born. It appears to me your Honor, that the defendant's got quite a few children, identities and quite a few stories to go along with it. The government believes that Mr. Patterson will be a flight risk, and we aren't sure that he wasn't involved in the murders of a Baltimore police officer, who was undercover and dating his daughter's mother......."

"Objection! Your Honor, we've been over this a million times and I was informed by the agents who are investigating this case that my client is not a suspect in these cases, in fact, my client was in San Francisco visiting with his wife's mother who was in the hospital when this happened and further, my client only had a 'buy and sell' relationship with the suspect wanted in the shooting of the FBI Agent and the murder of the police officer was a robbery in the mall that was caught on tape. It appeared to be a random robbery that went bad your Honor. Again, my client was nowhere around at the time."

This guy was really earning his $50,000.00 that Steph was paying that I knew I would be repaying some day. Nothing came without a price, not in this life. The judge was somewhat amused with my attorney's performance because he seemed to be siding with the defense to some degree.

The Court even surprised me when he stated, "I've heard quite a bit about the defendant Mr. Patterson and Frankly I think the government has failed to carry its burden...."

The prosecutor realized that she was about to lose and quickly added "Your Honor, as I mentioned earlier, the defendant may not have been around when the murders were committed but that doesn't mean that he's not involved and to make matters worse, your Honor, the defendant refuses to cooperate. Therefore, the government asks that the defendant be detained."

I hate when the prosecutor is a woman, they seem to have so much to prove and the judges love them. I could see all the questions on both Brishette and China's face when the prosecutor told them about another baby being born because neither of them knew about Candice.

"Your Honor, my client has not been charged with any murders or any violent crimes for that matter. I object to the government's use of such information as a basis in opposing release pending trial."

"Mrs. McNally, I didn't ask you what you thought, I asked you did he qualify as a flight risk or threat to society. You have the Federal code and rules in front of you, tell me what the book says, not what you think."

"Your Honor...." the judge began to get tired of the prosecutions antics.

"Do you have his passport?"

"Yes, your Honor, but......."

"Just answer the question Mrs. McNally."

I looked back at China and got a dirty look back. Probably because my secret child was now out in the open. I'd now have to explain to both Brishette and China about Candy an unintentional fling. I really didn't plan on getting Candy pregnant. One thing for sure, I definitely can't take it back. What's done is done and even though I didn't intend for this to happen, it did. So now I have to take care of my children, all of them.

CHAPTER 19

VERY EVEIL IF YOU CROSS ME

The judge obviously either didn't like the prosecutor or was a good friend of my lawyers because he gave me thirty days to get my affairs in order. After my lawyers convinced me to plead guilty to 36 months, my sentencing date was set off for 3 months. So, they called the release of pre-sentence conditional release, a sort of stay of execution or at least that's what the state should have called it.

I got processed and released later that evening around 8:00p.m. That was another thing that had me puzzled. Why don't they just release you from the courthouse anymore? Now you have to go all the way back to jail and get processed along with the rest of the people being released that day from doing sentences.

Brishette arrived around 8:40p.m. I got into the car and the first thing I heard was "Dee, why didn't you tell me about the children that you have all over the place?" I feel like a fool, like you just played me......"

"Hold up! I don't get no hello, how are you doing, I miss you or nothing?"

The look in her eyes was one I'd never seen before, it was cold and dark, and her words spoke volumes more than what she actually said.

"Let's get one thing straight before we go any further, Dee, there's a lot about me I haven't told you yet, just like it's a lot you haven't told me."

"Like what?" I studied her eyes and body language as I spoke. I saw something different about her this night, something that made me very curious.

"Dee, I've been hurt many times and I'm not the sweet Brishette you know when I'm hurt and betrayed......"

I didn't like the way this was going so I cut her off. "So, what are you trying to tell me?"

"I'm just asking you not to hurt me anymore. Dee, I was crushed when I heard you had some other woman pregnant here in L.A., so that means you were cheating on me, and I thought you were different."

"First, let's get the hell away from this prison or let me drive."

"Dee, I need you to know that I can be very evil if you cross me. All I ask is that from now on, please be honest with me about everything because I rather hear the truth than a lie, cause that would mean I can't trust you. We don't need to be married if there's no trust, that's all I'm saying. Oh yeah, that girl Candice has a big mouth, she told the nurse all her business, how she met you and how you stayed at her house. I know all about that......"

"Hold up, how do you know all of that?"

"My sister's best friend works at the hospital, they gossip Dee."

Damn, this is crazy. How, in a million years, can some shit like this happen to me. Now that I think about it that explains the looks. I knew it was something deep.

"Brissh look, that was about the time I...."

She cut me off.... "Around the time you were staying with her, I know." Brishette coolly stated with piercing eye contact.

"That was before I fell in love with you Brish. It was something that just happened. What you need to keep in mind is that I married you because I want to spend the rest of my life with you, despite my past. This is not about our past, it's about our future. So, I need you to promise me one thing, that you will not question my love or loyalty to you again. I don't love easy, but when I do, I love for real and I'm a man of honor Brishette. Please don't ever forget that."

"Dee, let me explain something to you. I'm not as niave as people seem to think. I just didn't choose writing because I didn't know what else to do. I'm in this business because I wanted to write about some of my experiences. I was just fortunate to have someone in the

industry to help me connect with the right people. I should also tell
you that it is no coincidence that you got out on bond.
It was done as a favor to my uncle."
"Wait a minute, so you made that happen?"
"Let's just say it was a Hollywood favor. There's a lot you don't know
yet about me Dee."
"What's that supposed to mean? Before she could answer, my phone
came alive with its distinctive ring. "Hello"
"What's up partner?" The familiar voice crooned through the phone
seeking a response.
"Who is this? Mel?"
"Yeah, it's me youngster. I heard what happened to you and I cut the
girl off for that grimy shit she did. That's one thing I can't have around
me is a snitch. They make me want to do something to them. Yeah as
soon as your wife called me and told me what happened, I came to
court with her and Steph."
"I appreciate that Mel, " cutting my eyes over at Brishette, as we raced
through traffic.
"Aye youngster, I hope it ain't no hard feelings about the girl. She was
a snake anyway. She didn't like how tight we were and she wanted to
turn us against each other. So, I played along until I got it out of her,
that she had set you up......" Mel sounded sincere in his attempt to
reconcile our Reecee - induced differences. I will never forget what
Splizzy heard him say about somebody going home in a box.
"Yeah, she told me she done that shit."
"Awight youngster, I just wanted to tell you what's up and welcome
you home. So go ahead and enjoy yourself. And, oh yeah my
condolences to you and your family. I'm sorry to hear about your
baby's mother."
"Yeah, thanks. I appreciate everything Mel."
"I'll get at you tomorrow and tell your wife I said hello."
"Awight, peace." Silence filled the car as I stared out the window,
thinking about all that had happened in such little time. There was
definitely a lesson to be learned from all of this. I knew I needed to
get to my daughter, but not tonight. It would have to be first thing in
the morning.
I couldn't wait to get into a nice hot bathtub, get my back washed and

scrubbed at the same time by the softest hands in the world. The fleeting hands of my wife temporarily washing away the stress and pain of Rissa's death and the funeral arrangements that played in my mind. Brishette and I made passionate and careful love. Exhaustion over took us, falling asleep, comfortably cuddled so as not to hurt the baby.

CHAPTER 20

DO YOU KNOW WHO HER UNCLE IS

The next morning, I woke up somewhat refreshed, grateful that I was in the free world, in a real bed beside my French wife and baby. I took a 20 minute shower, letting the water run over my head, eyes closed, thinking about how I was going to take care of the transporting of Rissa's body back to Baltimore and the funeral arrangements without putting my name on any of it because I didn't need
any new charges of tax evasion or having them ask me a bunch of questions about where I got the money or any of that so I decided to get Lil Kim, my daughter's mother's sister to come out to California and help get her sister's body back and make arrangements for the funeral.
I entered the bedroom to get dressed and found Brishette frowning and holding her stomach, "You awight?" I asked out of concern, when seeing her face all balled up like she was in pain.
"Yeah, I guess I'm okay. The baby just kicked me, that's all. I brought you some things from the mall and I picked you some shoes from your apartment."
"Thank you baby, I appreciate it......" My phone began ringing on the night stand.
"Hand me that phone please."
I sat at the end of the bed listening while Brishette handed me the phone, "Hello."

"Dee, what's up? You enjoy your first night home? Ah man, that wife of yours got juice in this town. You didn't tell me you married a Hollywood insider. I gotta take my hat off to you partner because you sure know how to pick em. Do you know who her uncle is?"

"Naw, who?" I answered trying not to look her way to show her I was talking about her.

"I'll let you find out on your own."

"So what are you doing? It sounds like you doing a lot of moving around."

"I'm getting dressed and getting ready to get out of here, trying to make arrangements to get my daughter's mother's body back to Baltimore."

"Oh yeah man, I'm sorry to hear about your daughter's mother. Well get at me when you get done with everything, and if you need me, call me."

We hung up and I got dressed. Damn, it felt good to be home and to put on some real clothes and not that cold-assed short sleeved 2 piece V-neck prison uniform that they make you wear while freezing you to death with the air conditioner to keep you under submission and keep your mind off all that time they be giving out like it's candy. I couldn't help but think that whole night, who could have killed Rissa and why? And the only logical idea was the people who killed the police and if that was the case then maybe they were the ones who kidnapped Rissa and Isha. If so, then how much of this did Splizzy know about? Maybe it was a random robbery/kidnapping. Did he know it all? I also needed to get Lil Kim to come get the body. I quickly called Kim's number.

"Hello."

"Did I wake you?" It sounded as if she was asleep.

"No, I was just laying here, why what's up Dee?"

"Listen, I need you to pack an overnight bag and go the airport...."

Kim cut me off before I could finish, "Wait, wait...pack an overnight bag and go to the airport for what? Where am I going?"

"Kim, Rissa is dead, I need...."

"No, Noooooooo........" I could hear the pain as she cried out. "Oh, my God! What happened Dee?"

"We don't know yet, they found her body the other day. I was in jail when it happened, they just told me about it."

"In jail? What is going on? How could you let something happen to my sister? What about Isha, is she okay? Oh my God, my father is going to have a heart attack.."

"Isha is fine. Look, we'll talk more when you get here. I just need you right now."

"It must have suddenly hit her, because she put the phone down and started crying really loud. "Imma call you back Dee, let me get myself together." She sobbed into the phone without another word.

I then contacted Northwest Airlines, and had Brishette pre-pay the round trip ticket

from B.W.I. Airport to L.A.X. In the name Kimberly Grant. with a credit card.

By this time, I had gotten two voice mail messages from Splizzy and surprisingly, one from Twyla and even more surprisingly, one from Jay's brother Kevin. I was more curious as to why Kevin had called. So I called the number he had left and a girl answered.

"Hello."

"Hello, can I speak to Kevin?"

"Who's calling?"

"Tell him it's Dee returning his call," I could hear her calling him in the background.

"Hello?"

"What's up Kev?"

"Aye, what's going on partner? I ain't heard from you in a while, is everything alright? I really called you cause I got a message for you, but I need to see you in person, so where you at now?"

I was not comfortable with trusting anybody, especially after the kidnapping and murder of my daughter's mother, but my gut feeling was that Jay or Kevin was not involved. If they were, how did they know about Isha and Rissa, and what would be their motive for killing Rissa and kidnapping Isha?

It just don't seem like nothing they would do. So I decided to meet Kevin to see what's up. Maybe he had information about the case and how I could beat it or maybe Jay was trying to contact me. "I'm in L.A."

"Awight bet, check this out. There's a small coffee Bistro-like spot in

Neiman Marcus on Rodeo Drive. Just take the elevator to the 2nd level. I'll be there around noon."

"Hold-up, I don't know if I can make it that soon. I got some things I need to take care of. My daughter's mother came out here to visit with my daughter and somebody murdered her."

"What? Man that's crazy, murdered which one? The mother or the daughter?"

"Her mother."

"Damn, man I'm sorry to hear that Dee. So do they know how it happened? Did she know people out here or something?"

"Kev, I know about as much as you know. I was locked up when this happened."

"Locked up? For what? What happened?"

"We're gonna have to talk when we get together because I gotta get out of here and get to the spot to make arrangements for the body. So how do you want to do this? You want me to call you when I'm done?"

"Yeah, why don't you do that. Call me when you're ready to meet and I'll tell you where to meet me."

CHAPTER 21

THE BODY

Brishette had an early morning meeting with a Sony Producer; that I insisted she go back to. I needed to handle this alone so she dropped me off at the funeral home in Inglewood on Manchester near the forum and headed back into L.A. Steph had set it up for me to meet the owner, a tall midnight black flashy man with a beer, collard greens, chicken and cornbread-gut.

"You must be DeJohn," he stated as he entered the visiting area wearing a quality black suit, white shirt and black tie, like the Men in Black. You could tell he was from the hood. He wore gold rings on almost every finger as if he was a loan shark for crackheads.

"Yeah, you must be Karl," I said somewhat sarcastically, extending my hand.

"First, let me get Pamela, my daughter, she can accommodate any dressing requests that you might have so that the body will be ready for viewing shortly after arriving in Baltimore, or you could let them do it. But, I suggest you let her take care of everything here. Excuse me just a minute. He had a distinctive limp as if one of his legs was longer than the other or something as he disappeared down the dimly-lit, spooky hallway.

I hated the funeral homes; especially after seeing all the scary, spooky-assed shit on T.V.. I was expecting some fat, sloppy, 300lb girl or a less attractive daughter. She must have been adopted or

something because she looked nothing like her burnt crisp father. "Hi, I'm Pam," she reached out to shake my hand, showing off her wedding ring. "Follow me, let me show you the body."
Damn, this was the part I didn't like. I didn't like looking at no damn bodies unless they were beautiful, alive and naked. We walked into a cold well-lit room and the scent of chemicals smacked me in the face. This smell reminded me of my cousin Junebug; back when we were little sitting on the steps. His ass stayed with a bag up to his face filled with glue or turpentine or whatever he could find to get his inhalant high on. That's why he lost his damn mind and thought he was jumping in a pool when he jumped into the Druid Hill Park Reservoir. They say the current was so strong, it sucked him right under. He didn't have a chance, even if he wasn't high out of his mind. I could feel the knots in my stomach start to come alive, like I'd been running a marathon. She pulled the body out and pulled the sheet back, she was butt-naked. "Was she like this when they found her?" I wondered whether she had been raped.
"I'm not sure, you see we don't get the body first. The coroner's office picks up the body from the scene; then after they're done, we get the body. I'm really sorry about your loss."
"Yeah thanks. You can cover her back up now." My phone began it's distinctive chiming. "Excuse me, I have to take this." I said walking out of that gloomy assed room.
I can't see how the fuck people can work around dead bodies, I thought as I answered Kim's call. "Hello, speak to me."
"Dee, I'm at the airport getting ready to board the plane. I had a little problem getting the ticket because I had accidentally left my I.D., or my girlfriend Yaya's hot-assed lil sister had it. She met me at the airport and brought it to me, so I got it and I'm on my way. I'll call you when I get there and land. Awight, Love you."
"Awight, I'll send somebody to get you or I might be there myself." The undertaker girl was pointing to the front hinting that that's where she'd be when I finished my call. "Kim, I gotta go, I'll see you when you get here." I followed her to the front office where she started adding up everything with and without her dressing the body. I decided to let them dress Rissa, but I told her that I'd like to let her sister choose what she should wear home. She should be here by

4:00p.m.and as soon as she gets here I'll bring her by so you and she can then work out everything. I paid her and got the hell out of there. My stomach was fucked up, the stench in the air, the way my mouth dried up had my tongue sticking to the roof of my mouth. My hands were sweaty. I almost felt like if I would have stayed there a little longer, Rissa would jump up and tried to fight me for letting some shit like this happen to her. I walked out like I had a car parked out there. I had forgotten that Brishette had dropped me off.

I called Steph, he asked me was I finished.

"Yeah, come get me the fuck away from here."

"Yo Dee, are you awright? You don't sound too good."

"Ah yo, just hurry up and get me the fuck from around here. I hate funeral homes, yo."

"What's the ad..........."

I didn't even let him finish that dumb-assed shit. "Man, where the fuck you at man?"

"Yo, calm down. I'm about 10 minutes from you."

"Yo, Steph. I'm a be walking down Manchester towards the gas station."

"Awight, I got you, be right there."

The whole time I walked I couldn't think of nothing but who the fuck.....Damn. It seemed like every other car that drove pass me look like Rissa in the car. Damn, I was tripping. I gotta find out who did this shit to Rissa. My mind won't rest until I do. The horn startled me as Steph pulled up to the curb and brought me out of my deep thoughts.

"Dee!" I turned and immediately noticed that he had a new whip. A metallic sparkling-silver Maserati with gray leather and wood grain dash, console and steering wheel. I quickly hopped in. He turned down the Mariah Carey joint he was listening to and before he could say anything I asked about the whip, " Damn, Steph you switching up cars like that now?"

"Oh, I ordered this a while back. They just got it in. I always wanted one of these Dee. You only live once ya know. So, you awight? Is everything straight? Did the dude Karl take good care of you?"

"Yeah, everything is straight except what she gone wear, but I got her sister on the way out here from Baltimore. Her flight gets in around

4o'clock. I gotta pick her up and let her take care of all that and get the body back to Baltimore. I appreciate you putting that together for me because I wouldn't have known where to go, not being from out here."

"That's the least I could do."

We were now on the 10 freeway in the fast lane rolling. "I was just with somebody that wants to see you. Man this girl is crazy about you."

"What girl?" now he had me curious.

"You'll see, we meeting them for breakfast. We'll be there in a minute." the car became silent for the rest of the ride with the exception of Luther's "House is not a home," bringing back memories of my old girl Shelly, who used to love me to death. She was sixteen and I was eighteen. She had a body to die for or kill for. Damn, its funny how songs bring back old thoughts and feelings. I loved the shit out of her and still do, but I can't get out of my mind that she killed our baby. Damn, we would've had a beautiful baby. She was definitely a model in her own right. She was sexy as hell, her almond brown skin, that million dollar smile and that look of seduction. I guess she was about a 34B with Chinese perky breast. Her ass was perfect. Damn I miss her and we almost got back together except that she didn't believe in me. I told her that I was gonna make all her dreams come true but she made me feel like a trick when she told me I couldn't get no pussy until I bought her a house. That's fucked up. Then we started to slowly slip apart and soon after that I saw my opportunity to do my thing and blew up. Buying four cars in less than two months, so I could switch up. Living on the beach and shit.

Chapter 22

TRIAD GANG CALLED 14K

I was glad when we pulled up in the parking lot of I.H.O.P. We were
on Hawthorne Boulevard. You could see Nordstrom's not far away."
As we walked inside, I began scanning the restaurant for familiar
faces. I saw no one until we walked around to the other side of the
Horse-shoe layout and then I saw China, Isha and Splizz.
"Hey Daddy." I reached down putting my arms around my daughter's
shoulders resting my chin on her small head.
"Hey Isha, how is daddy's big girl? You okay?
"Yes, I missed you Daddy."
"Yeah, she talked me to sleep about you last night. I called myself
tucking her in with a bed time story and she instead had me yawning,
but she's good company and a little trooper too!" China exclaimed.
"Oh yeah," I said pulling up a chair between China and Isha. "So,
what's up Splizz?" What's really going on and how did you all hook
up to make this little reunion happen?"
"We are your family. You know we was gonna be here for you when
you needed us," Splizzy said waving over the hostess. "You hungry?"
"Yeah, a little bit."
"You know we need to talk right?" China stated with a piercing stare
of seriousness. I knew exactly what she wanted to talk about, but it
was not the time.
My phone began ringing. "I need to get this excuse me," I got up and
walked away toward the front. "Hello?"

"DeJohn, this is Ms. Helen, how you doing baby?"

"Oh hey, Ms. Hellen. I almost didn't recognize your voice. You sound different."

"That's because I ain't slept since I heard the news. What is that little girl going to do without her mother? My grand baby loves her some mommy, so how is she holding up?"

"She's holding up pretty good so far Ms. Hellen."

"Oh yeah, your mother been by here. She sat with us for a good while and she says that she ain't heard from you since you and her had an argument about one of those girls. Now you know that ain't right. That's your mother and no matter what, you only get one. So you better treat her right while you got her cause you never know when God's gone bring her home. You know what I mean baby?"

"Yes maam."

"Where's my grand baby? Put her on the phone." I started walking back to the table. "Hold on, let me get her." I walked towards the table calling out to Isha, "Isha, here" I handed her the phone.

"Who is it Daddy?"

"Your grandmother."

China was looking so good, as usual. She wore a Banana ice cream yellow Gucci tee with matching yellow capri pants and accenting Gucci sandals. She even had the yellow toe-nail polish, and tortoiseshell Gucci shades setting it off. While I was still standing and my daughter distracted by the telephone conversation, China made her move. She grabbed me by my arm leading me away from the table. "Dee, I really need to talk to you, it's important."

I turned and shouted, "I'll be right back," almost being pulled away. We stepped outside the restaurant and took a seat on the benches in front.

"Dee, I've been trying to tell you this since we were together at the new mansion, the same night you got the call that your daughter and her mother had been kidnapped, but it wasn't the right time."

"Right time for what China, what's on your mind, because whatever it is, it's got your attention."

"I don't think I talked to you about my uncle in Hong Kong, but he's into a little bit of everything and when I say everything, I MEAN EVERYTHING!"

"so, why you telling me about your uncle in China, I don't get it?"

"That's because I'm not finished." she stated somewhat sarcastically.
"The reason I bring him up is he's been trying to get me involved in
his international travel agency ring. Well he uses his travel agencies
as a conduit for a very big escort service, which is just a front for the
prostitution that has made my family so rich and powerful in China
and other countries as well."

"I don't get it China. So why were you an exotic dancer when you
could be a lawyer or doctor or something, if your family got money?"

"I did it because I wanted to, it had nothing to do with money. I just
felt freedom when I danced."

"What do you mean freedom?"

"It's a long story Dee, plus you wouldn't understand anyway."

"You'd be surprised. Give me the short version and try me."

"Look Dee, my mother was the only girl in a Hong Kong family of all
boys who were all members of a Triad Gang called 14K. They were so
protective of their baby sister that she couldn't live a normal life, have
boyfriends, see who she wanted, nor go where she wanted. There
was always the fear of her dating a rival or being kidnapped or killed.
So my mother came to the United States to go to college. My family
spoiled her and because she lived such a sheltered-prisoner type of
life in China, she became adventurous and started going to parties,
drinking and whatever else she could get into. Well, a long story
short, she started to date a few guys outside her race. Anyway, when
she returned back home she learned that she was pregnant. She
didn't know which of the guys she slept with was the father. She had
the baby and my family learned that the father was a black man.
In Hong Kong, your family lost respect if it was found out that you
mixed blood with another culture or race so I became the family's
secret. I could not go out, I couldn't play with other children. I was a
miserable child. Then my mother decided it was too much for me so I
was sent to live with family in San Francisco's China town. They were
very protective. I got sick of it so when I turned 18, I came to Los
Angeles to go to school. I've just been seeking my own identity and
freedom. I also wanted to show my family that I don't need their
money or gang's protection. Anyway, that's enough for now, let's get
back inside before your daughter think we left her."

"Yeah, plus I gotta get somebody to pick up my daughter's mother's sister from the airport. Can you take care of that for me? And I have one question, where is your mother and father?"

As we walked inside China explained that her mother died in a plane crash and she never got to meet her father because the Triads forbade her mother from seeing him again. Damn, I never knew any of this shit. So how is her uncle going to take me as his niece's Black partner?

"So, have you told your uncle about me?"

"No, not yet, but I figured as long as I'm not pregnant and he sees the major potential I have with you as my partner, they'll be fine. I've thought about it a lot and it's just perfect for what we are doing. Look Dee, the travel agencies are everywhere and they move beautiful women all around the world. Like our girls can be sent there on vacation and the world's most beautiful Asian and Russian girls are sent here in sort of a rotation. Keeping new and exciting exotic girls coming and going. Think of what it would do to our mansion parties and V.I.P. Business. If you think about it we'd get all the money the clubs get for the dancers, but tenfold."

"Daddy, where did you go? My grand mommy wanted to speak back to you. She said call her back."

"Okay baby." Damn, China had my mind racing about all that money we could be making, but of course, I needed to know more before I jumped in.

CHAPTER 23

THE BEATDOWN

I was surprised, but pleased, to hear that Mel had kept his word when he said that he was so mad when he found out that Reecee set me up that he was going to make sure that she got hers. In fact, it made me smile to hear that he paid some girls to wait for her outside the nail salon on Crenshaw. He said that when she came out, one of the girls sprayed her face with mace and they beat her down and got to stomping her in between two cars. She managed to get away from them, but not away from the water truck that hit her knocking her into the air. The girls didn't stick around to see if she lived or died, but they told me it wasn't pretty. I ended that call with a puzzled look on my face because Karma had performed immediate retribution and I didn't have to lift a finger. So it's true that what you do to somebody else, will come back to you ten-fold. I just wanted her to be taught a lesson and now she might be dead. I couldn't call Candy and ask about her sister because she's gonna wonder how I knew about it.

We left the restaurant and all headed back to the mansion. During the ride back, I noticed Splizzy wasn't his talkative self. I've known him practically all his life and I know when something is up. Either he is going through something or he's up to something. The only way I'd ever know is to ask. "So, what's going on with you Splizz?" I leaned up from the back seat, putting my arms around the two front seats, so I could see his expression while he sat shotgun while China drove. "Ain't nothing, just chillin, you know just thinking about everything, that's all."

"You've been quiet most of the morning and that isn't like you. You're usually the life of the party. So what's on your mind?" Before he could answer, my phone rang, this time it was my mother. I knew I'd have to face her sooner or later.

"Hello." I braced myself expecting her to curse me out for not calling her.

"DeJohn, I'm really sorry to hear about Rissa. I know that must be hard on you and Nisha. I just wanted you to know that I'm here for you. So, if you need me to cook or help out somehow with the funeral or watch Isha or whatever, just let me know, okay?"

"Ma, I appreciate that. I guess you could get with Ms. Hellen and see what she needs, but I don't even know if these people gone let me come back to Baltimore or not. I have to find out because in court the lawyer kept talking about me getting out to make funeral arrangements, but he never said to the court that I needed to go back."

"Wait a minute, what are you talking about DeJohn? Where are you right now?" She said cutting me off. "I'm in California Ma, I've been out here for a while."

"I know you were in California, Hellen told me that, but nobody told me anything about a court. So what have you done now? You in some kind of trouble ain't chew? Well, please don't ask me to come to no court house and all that because I'm just sick and tired of it. You got a hard head and a hard head make a soft ass. You need to..........................."

"Ma! Ma!" I had to cut her off or she would have went on and on. "I'm fine. I don't need you to come no where Ma. I'm good! I don't need this right now. You said you wanna help, well you not helping right now."

"Boy don't you get smart with me. I'm just saying, when are you going to stop getting in trouble and where's that baby at?"

"She's right here Ma. She fell asleep laying across my lap."

"So why haven't you called me? I know you ain't still mad about some damn girl."

"Aye Ma, I don't want to talk about that."

"I guess you don't want to talk about it. You know that wasn't right about what you did to that girl Monica. That girl is crazy about you and so is that lil boy of yours. She's the best thing that ever happened to you.

You damn right I told her you was cheating on her. You're just like your father before he died, the best ain't never enough for yall kind of people. That's right I told her she need to move on and find somebody that will make her happy........."

I couldn't take it no more. "Ma I gotta go. I'm hanging up."

"You better not hang up this phone while I'm talking to you DeJohn."

"Aye Ma, I gotta go. I got another call coming in on the other line, hold on."

"Hello." It was Brishette.

"Hey baby, where are you? Are you still at the funeral home?"

"No, I'm headed towards Santa Barbara right now."

"Oh, okay. I thought we might have had a chance to do lunch together, but..........."

"Hold on, let me tell my mother I'll call her back."

"No, you go ahead and talk with your mom. Just call me back when you get time. I was just calling to check on you. Make sure you were okay....."

"Alright, I'll call you back." I clicked back to my mother. "Ma, I'm gonna have to get back to you."

"I'll be here. If I leave out, I'm only going to the grocery store."

"Alright. I'll talk to you later."

CHAPTER 24

I LEARNED FROM THE BEST

As we traveled the coastline nearing the new mansion's Santa Barbara location, I couldn't help but think of the drama that surrounded me right now. My daughter was mother-less, my wife pregnant, I'm about to go to prison, I just found out that my partner China is the niece of a Chinese family of Triad Drug Lords,and my best friend is on some brand new sit and that ain't good. Then after all the shit I've been through with Reecee, I couldn't believe she set me up. I feel like Rissa's death is my fault. This could have gone a totally different direction.

This was the first time I had the chance to see China's work. The mansion was all that I expected and more. I guess, because it was Santa Barbara, it was huge. The first thing I noticed was the 8 car garage as we pulled into the garage. We then took an elevator to the first floor, just outside of a study.

"Dog, China," I tried to watch my language around Isha as much as possible, "Girl, you did your thing didn't you?"

"What can I say, I learned from the best."

"Daddy, you wanna play video games with me?"

"Not right now baby, but maybe later okay?"

"Ms. China, can I go play the video game?"

"It's okay with me, but you have to ask your daddy, Isha."

"It's okay Isha, go ahead." She took off into the living room.

"Dee, I'll be back. I gotta make a run real fast." Splizzy stated coming down the hall, "Plus, you probably need some time to talk, if you want I'll take Isha with me."

"Naw, that's awright. She's good." I refused looking at China to see what her response was. Maybe they planned this, I don't know. All I know was Splizzy was acting strange. I hope they ain't sleep together. Whatever it is, it'll come out soon. I knew if I was left alone with China, she might tempt me, so I decided to play it safe and keep Isha around.

I'm a married man now and I'm gonna try to control my sexual addictions.

"Dee, you wanna come up and let me show you around?"

"Right now, I just want a drink. I'm stressed out, China!"

"Come on, the bar is in the downstairs lavender room. There's one upstairs also." China explained as if I was going to complain or something about her lavender rooms.

"The lavender room?"

"Yeah, it's my favorite color and it is scientifically proven to relax you. Some even say it is medicinal or therapeutic. The Chinese use it to heal."

I must admit, I was impressed. She had retracted lighting, white tables, and the art deco furniture did remind me of a club or lounge-like setting. I kept getting flashbacks or our last time together in Jamaica, where we shared Twyla. She had fulfilled one of my fantasies and I would never forget it.

We sat down near a full length Bay window overlooking the huge pool. The sun permeated the room and offered the right amount of illumination. "Dee, I don't know what to do." China purred resting her head on my shoulder as if to seek refuge.

"You don't know what to do about what, China?" I turned slightly to my left to meet her seductive but saddened gaze. "About you Dee, what am I gonna do without you?"

"You're gonna do fine China, just like you've done so far without me around. Look at this place, you picked this all by yourself. You're getting ready to take this thing to another level and I'll be proud of you China. How many of your friends besides Lashanda can you say is doing it big like you are.?"

"It's just not going to be right Dee without you right here."

I put my arm around China and tilted my head to meet hers. It felt good to have a real friend that I could share so much with.

"Dee, I'm a mess right now. I feel like I'm in love with you like you're my husband or something and you're leaving me. It's crazy because you are somebody else's husband. I kind of like her too Dee. She's probably good for you. We had a long talk about you. We had lunch and kicked it for a while. I don't know what I'm feeling. I don't know whether I'm jealous or happy for you two. Then she's pregnant, that means whether you stay with her or not, she'll always have a part of you with her."

My phone rang and interrupted us, "Excuse me, Hello."

"Dee, this is Kim. I'm almost there. They said it should be about another hour or so. Okay, I gotta get off of this phone, it's expensive."

"Awright Kim. Somebody will be there to pick you up. I'll see you when you get here."

"Okay, bye."

"That was my baby mother's sister. You got somebody to go get her from the airport, right?"

"Yeah, I already talked to Lonia....."

"Lonia? Who is that?"

"Appolonia, she's one of our girls. She's a sweet girl. She helps me out some times. You'll meet her, in fact, let me call her and find out where she is. She did tell me that she'd be at her mother's over in Inglewood right near the airport. So she'll be on it. So what time is her flight so I can have her there waiting?"

"She said around 4o'clock....." My phone came to life once again with its distinctive ring. "Hello?"

"Dee, it's Kevin, where you at? I need to see you now! It's getting late and I gotta go out of town. Everything awight? I've been trying to get with you since this morning man. We need to talk in person. Look, this is what I need you to do, in 30 minutes, be at a pay phone. I'm gonna call you back and give you the number to a pay phone and you call me right back from your pay phone and I'll tell you where to meet me."

"Hold on. Aye China, where's the nearest pay phone?"

"It's about ten minutes from here, why what's wrong?"

"Awight Kev. I'll wait for your call. I'm leaving in a few minutes."

As we hung up, my mind began racing to questions then conclusions. First, I wondered did he know I got locked up and I was now out on bond. Second , I wondered had they caught Jay and he was trying to get a message to me about what to say. It's got to be something about Jay because the Feds already got me. Damn, what if they're trying to set me up to have me murdered thinking that I might snitch?

CHAPTER 25

BY YOURSELF RIGHT?

"Dee, I got Lonia on the Phone, so what's the girl's name?" China said to me, holding the phone down at her side.

"Her name is Kimberly Grant and it's Northwest Airlines. Oh yeah, she needs to go straight to the funeral home so they can work out the details on what they are gonna dress Rissa in."

"I don't know how much time she's gonna have but I'll ask her for you."

"I need you to make that happen because I gotta go meet up with my man, Kev.

We pulled up to a bar called "The Lady Blue" 10 minutes from the estate along the shoreline of Coastal Route 101. China walked inside just ahead of me. The stench of a cheap disinfectant failing to cover up the combination of stale liquor, urine from the over-used and under-cleaned restroom, mixed with years of body odors lashed out as us. The dim lighting added to its gloomy atmosphere, within seconds of reaching the bartender, my cell phone began to ring.

"Excuse me sir, where is your pay phone?"

"It's right around the corner, on your left by the restrooms. If you have a problem with the other person hearing you just tap the receiver against the wall."

That's just what I needed, to be near the source of the odor that caused my stomach to turn. I quickly located the pay phone, leaving China at the bar ordering a Coke.

I dialed the number. "Hello?"

"Yeah, take this number down."

"Go ahead, I'm ready."

"310-555-7005. Call me right back."

I dialed the number from the pay phone and began rubbing the smelly receiver against my pants leg. Kevin obviously answered on the first ring because he was on the phone when I put the receiver to my ear.

"Hello."

"Yeah, I'm here. Where you at?"

"I'm about 45 minutes from L. A."

"45 minutes? Where da fuck you at man?"

"I'm out near the beach......"

"The beach? Never mind, uhmmmm....You know where the Holiday Inn Rooftop Restaurant is?"

"Yeah...."

"Meet me there, I'll spot you when you walk in. So how long you gone be?"

"I'm on my way."

"Hey, you coming by yourself right?"

"I got my girl with me."

"Yeah awight, I'll see you when you get here."

The crazy part about all of this is I still don't know who's responsible for the kidnapping of my daughter and the murder of her mother. All sorts of shit was going through my head at this point. It could be anyone of several people. It could be Mel or he could have something to do with it, especially since he was found in my house with Reecee and China heard him say something about sending my family home in a box. How do I really know that he had Reecee beat down because she set me up? She could have just got hit by a car crossing the street. Then there was Jay. I had to wonder whether he'd want to get rid of me because I might talk, but they wanted him for killing an F.B.I. Agent not me. I had nothing to do with that. In fact, I wasn't even around. Maybe it really did have something to do with the murder of that agent. Maybe she was dating somebody on the F.B.I. team. Maybe he wanted some revenge by killing someone close to either one of us or whoever he could get to first. Sitting in that hotel room, unable to leave during the murder investigation had made Rissa a sitting duck. Then it could have had something to do with Rissa seeing one of the murderers who killed the Baltimore City Detective that posed as her boyfriend to trying to get me.

It was somewhat comforting that Kevin or Kev - as I called him -

asked that we meet in a public place like the Holiday Inn, where there are plenty of cameras in and out. What wasn't as comforting is that I don't know what the hell was going on in L.A.. The hotel parking lot was full and we had to find parking on the street or just sit around until someone left and we had already kept Kevin waiting for an hour. As we entered the semi-crowded elevator, my phone did its distinctive ring. I don't know which was more distracting, the surprise call from my son D.J.'s mother, Zelda, or flashbacks of the memorable threesome I enjoyed with Twyla and China in Jamaica when the suddenly full elevator caused China to squeeze back forcing her ass to make soft direct contact with my previously dormant manhood.

CHAPTER 26

YOU'VE GOT GOOD TASTE

"Hello."
"What's up DeJohn? I just got off the phone with your mother. She told me your daughter's mother got killed. I'm sorry to hear that." She was lying her ass off. She couldn't stand Rissa. As a matter of fact, Zelda was at a surprise birthday party my cousin J-rock threw for me on my 21st birthday and some kind of way Rissa must have had some beer go down the wrong pipe or something and started choking. Zelda said some crazy shit like, "I hope that bitch choke to death." As I remembered, that's what started their first fight back then and they couldn't stand each other every since.
"Yeah, I bet you are," I returned with a dose from my duffle bag of sarcasm.
"Naw, for real DeJohn. I ain't have nothing against her."
"Just that she had the daughter you really wanted," I stated as the elevator released us to the glitzy pre-evening happy hour crowd of the elegant rooftop experience that has made the restaurant a long time favorite and tourist attraction overlooking the Hollywood scene.
"Zel, I'll call you back." Just then China gave me that look.
"Wait, your mother said you were in California and that you got your daughter with you right? So why you ain't come get your son and take him too?"
"Her mother brought her out here Zelda."
"So why didn't you take us? Me and your son?"
"Look, I gotta go. I'll call you back. I'm getting ready to go in a meeting."
"Oh, now you all important and shit? Yeah right, whatever."
I spotted Kevin sitting at a table to the left of the bar. As China and I approached, I saw the look he gave China.
"Dee, who's your friend?" Kevin stood to greet us.
"This is my girl and business partner China. China, this is Kevin.
"Damn, you must have come straight out of Vogue. It's nice to meet you. Dee, you got good taste. She's a real dime piece."

Kevin held up China's hand getting ready to try that corny-assed hand kissing thing until China pulled her hand back from him.

"It's nice to meet you too, but I'm gonna leave you two for a while. I have to use the ladies room and make a few calls. Dee, I'm going to check on the airport situation and the other thing with the funeral home. I'll be back shortly."

China impressed me with the way she handled business and men. She had the right blend of sultry -but -toughness. She was always in control. She never let anybody cross the line. She never mentioned it but coming from a family of China's Chinese Triads, she was probably a black belt and would hurt or kill somebody if it came down to it. Damn, she had all the qualities of a "Bonnie." I felt like punching Kevin in his face because of his trance-like stares fixed on China's ass as she sashayed out of the restaurant. He had me hot. I was feeling like he was disrespecting me and it left me wondering what did I actually really feel for China.

I broke the monotony and got the focus off of China and back on business. "So, what's up Kev? Before she comes back."

"I'm supposed to pick you up and take you with me to see Jay. So as soon as your girl come back tell her you gonna ride with me."

"Oh yeah, so everything is awight then? They didn't....."

He cut me off as if he didn't want me talking about that. "Yeah, you want a drink or something before we get on the road? Plus, I need to ask you do you think anybody followed you here?"

"Follow me for what?"

"C'mon Dee, you sharper than that partner. They could have let you out just so you can lead them to where they want to be."

"Naw, I didn't notice anybody following us." My phone interrupted our conversation.

"Hello."

"Dee, what's up? It's Steph, Where you at?"

"I'm getting ready to go out of town with Kev. Why? What's going on Steph?"

"Tell Kev I said what's up. Look, just get at me as soon as possible. I got something real important to tell you. I just got off the phone with my people's and I don't like what I heard."

"Heard about what? What are you talking about?"

"Dee, I don't want to talk about this over the phone. Get at me when you get back because this is important. You need to hear this. So get at me."

"Yeah, awight. I'll call you when I get back."

China returned to the table and confirmed that Kim had been picked up and was now at the funeral home. I explained that I had to go out of town with Kevin and to make sure everything was taken care of with Kim and to take her to the mansion and I would come by as soon as I get back.

CHAPTER 27

YOUR NAME IS RINGING

During the four hour drive to Palm Springs, the sunset, palm trees, and old school CD's Kevin selected from his CD changer, like the O'Jays, "For The Love Of Money and Family Reunion" not to mention Stevie Wonder's "Ribbon In The Sky, and Earth, Wind and Fire's "Serpentine Fire," were all soothing, but not enough to keep my mind off of all the drama that surrounded my life.

I had just had a brand new baby by Candy, my wife was due to deliver any day, and to top it off, Reecee claimed she was pregnant too. Next, I'm having to deal with the death of my daughter's mother; the fake-assed sudden interest of my son's mother back in Baltimore. She probably just wanted to get back at Rissa, dead or alive for taking me from her and all the embarrassing ass-whippings Rissa repeatedly gave her over me.

We passed some beautiful homes that for some reason made me feel incomplete. Although I owned a mansion and a home in Jamaica, it was not enough because neither one of them could be called home - maybe homes away from home - but not home. I always wanted a family, all under one roof; especially after watching my mother and father separate. I realized later in life that that shit crushed me and my sister. I promised myself that when I had my own family, I would keep it together for my children to keep them mentally stable.

We arrived at, what the people in California called, a millionaire's flat. It was a well-lit gated community of nothing but multi-million

dollar homes. A gorgeous snow bunny answered the door and led Kevin and I to the kitchen where Jay was calling himself cooking. "Ya'll are just in time, I'm almost finished. So, what's going on Dee? How you been man?" We embraced while shaking.

"I'm good Jay. In spite of it all, you know me. I'm a survivor, you know."

"Yeah, so what's going on with them people? What did they charge you with?"

"They didn't know what to charge me with so they charged me with attempted conspiracy cause they don't have any drugs and they don't have you."

"So what they say about me? You eat lamb right?"

"Yeah, I eat lamb. It's gotta be well done though. I know how you like your meat medium rare. I don't do the blood thing."

"So, what did they say about me?"

"They just keep asking me was I involved in the murder. I told them I don't know nothing about no murders and that I was out of town when the so-called murder happened. I saw it on T.V. Then they started asking me about my relationship with you. I just told them I invoke my Fifth Amendment Right. Anything else you need to holler at my attorney, and that was it. I know a little law. I knew that once I invoked my Fifth Amendment Right they could not continue questioning me."

"Yeah, I appreciate hearing that." Jay said as he turned from the frying pans sizzling lamb chops that he poured wine over, like he really had some Chef skills. "Of course you already know loyalty means everything to me and I needed to assure myself that you could hold your own because almost everybody I know that's in the Feds, somebody told on them."

"Yeah, well where I come from, the code is "Inclusion creates conspiracies, conspiracies create problems and problems need solutions by any means necessary. That's the code we live by in Baltimore."

This beautiful white girl came in the kitchen, "Hey, is dinner almost ready?"

"Yeah, another 10 minutes. Oh yeah, forgive my manners. Dee this is Megan, Megan, Dee."

Damn she was fine. Her lips reminded me of Angelina Jolie, her long reddish blonde hair laid flawlessly down her back almost pointing out her black girl ass, which made up for her small but perky breasts.

"Nice to meet you Megan."

"Oh you too Dee. Jay, Tracy is in the shower, she's coming."

"Tell her I said hurry up."

Kevin had disappeared leaving Jay and I to talk in private. I kept my guard up because I was taught to trust no one in this game or any other game for that matter. One of the greatest movies of all time, "The Godfather," dropped so many jewels, but what really stuck with me is the saying, "Keep your friends close and your enemies even closer."

"I see you do the white girl thing?"

"Who Megan? Naw, she's just a friend of my grey-girl Tracey."

"Grey-Girl?"

"Yeah, that's what we call them in California."

"You ain't never had a white girl? Ahhh man Dee, you don't know what you are missing. That's all I fuck with is grey girls. White girls love brothers, especially if they're rich. You wait til you see Tracey. She's a 12 on a scale of 1 to 10. Who knows, maybe I'll hook you up with Megan."

"Man, I got enough problems as it is, plus I got a wife now and three baby mothers."

"Shiiit, I hear you getting rich out there, so what's going on with all this mansion shit I'm hearing? Your name is ringing in them streets, that could be good and that could be bad."

"So what do you mean my name is ringing? What you hear about me?"

"It's like this, I know a lot of people and when people have a good time, they tell people about it and others brag about being ballers. The bottom line is nothing happens out there that don't get back to me. I know the boy you get the credit from and his people was at one of your parties."

"So, who is this guy?"

"That don't matter, what matters is that you keep your nose clean. I know the people charged you with attempted conspiracy and that's because they don't have anything. Their only witness is dead and they don't have any taped conversations or anything because if they did, they would have charged you with conspiracy. So what are they saying about what you're looking at?"

"They said three years or so if I took it. The lawyer said if I take it, I shut the case down. He said as long as they don't have you, they couldn't charge me with conspiracy. Plus, the Feds give you 1 year off and six months in a halfway house for taking the drug program. So, that's 18 months off. By the time I get there and wait a few months to get into the drug program, then spend 10 months in the program, it'll be time to get released. So I'm good."

"So you got this shit all figured out, huh?"

"Once I get sentenced, it'll probably take about four months to get transported on the U.S. Marshall's Con Air plane, then my man told me to look forward to about two to three weeks in a holdover either in Oklahoma or Atlanta before you get to whatever prison they designate you to. So with a 36 month sentence, I might have 30 months left when I get to prison. Take 18 months, plus the 10 months in the program, that's 28 months, that leaves a couple months. I can do this shit standing on my head."

"I'm glad to hear that because so many people talk that tough tony shit and when it comes down to it, they break down and cooperate with the Feds and get a whole lot of people fucked up in the process."

"Well that ain't something that you got to worry about with me. I live by the code and die by the code. So that's why you had me come here?"

"I had you........you know what? That's part of the reason I had you come here and the other part was to have you come and enjoy yourself before going to prison and let you know that I got your back on anything you need, you just let Kevin know. As a matter of fact, Megan is going to be your new friend. I will send her to visit you with any messages and she'll send money to your books. So, make sure your wife or girlfriends know that she is your business associate so she won't have no drama in the parking lot. You feel me? Also, after we eat, we gonna chill a little while in the Jacuzzi with Megan and Tracey and then I'll explain to you what happened so you'll know the truth because it didn't happen like they said it did."

CHAPTER 28

I DIDN'T KILL THE GIRL

We were interrupted by the girls. "Hey, baby." Tracey said as she wrapped her arms around Jay's waist, kissing the back of his neck. I could see why Jay said what he said about Tracey. She was like that! She had cinnamon colored hair in a long pony tail, medium height, high cheekbones, perky virgin like breast, with a three finger gap between her bathing suit. The perfect shape. Not to mention, her million dollar smile and the tight-fitting Mochino jeans and fitting BeBe tee. Her neck was adorned with a beautiful dain'ty gold link necklace with a diamond pendant and diamond princess cut stud earrings to match. She made you know that she was loved by the way she moved. I watched as Jay made it also known that he really cared for her as well. What I didn't know is that her friend Megan was somewhat assigned to me as she soon let me know by her touchy-feely behavior, rubbing her feet up my leg while we ate dinner and her intentional warming up to me.

We finished dinner and retired to the Jacuzzi. I couldn't stay very long but I had to find out what really happened so at least I would know the truth and not just what the government was saying about Jay. I knew he was a principled individual but I didn't think he would

kill a Federal agent if he didn't have to, so I needed to find this out.
The girls left us for a while so we could talk and was waiting to give
us the pleasures we desired. Jay got straight to the point.

"Check this out Dee, I didn't kill the girl."

"So what happened?"

"Man, she was in a room that she had no business in right, and my
main man Juko seen her coming out of the room where my safe was
and everybody had been told to stay away from that room. I wasn't
even there. What I heard was this....when he asked what she was
doing in there, she tells him none of his business, so he slaps her.
They start fighting. Juko keeps a gun on him at all times because he is
a registered bodyguard. So she goes for the gun probably thinking
that he's going to tell me about it and let me decide what to do, but
when she went for the gun he drew and busted on her, shooting her
two times; once in the stomach and once in the chest."

"So they don't know what happened?"

"Right. They just assume that I did it."

"You know it ain't that easy. They're gonna still lock me up for drugs
and try to put the murder on me because they don't have the
murderer or the murder weapon and I ain't tellin'em nothing."

"Yeah, I feel you. So just lay low man until the statute of limitations
run out. That's what my uncle did. He waited until the five years ran
out to surface and they couldn't do nothing to him because it was too
late. Oh yeah, but there's no limitations on murder but the drugs,
yeah."

"Hey you, I'm waiting for you." Megan said to me from the glass
sliding door where she stood in her white terrycloth robe.

"Dee, go ahead and enjoy yourself..."

"Yeah, okay I'm coming."

"Not yet you aren't, wait until I get my hands on you." She was
winking her eye and pointing and bending her index finger telling me
to come to her.

Megan went inside closing the door behind her. This hustler life has
always been the root of my sex addiction and the fact that I always
wanted a white girl and my wife is pregnant and I'm about to go to
federal prison, all were reasons enough to take this one last dance
and enjoy myself like there was no tomorrow. At least it might get

my mind off my daughter's mother's death for a hot minute. Her funeral would surely bring me back to reality, but for now, I'm gonna enjoy this brief fantasy-filled moment. I joined Megan in the shower, had her wash me as I washed her, taking extra care to make sure the pussy was real clean. She had the most beautiful breast that I took my time and sucked so intently making her so wet that I just glided inside of her as I raised one of her legs slightly over the rim of the bathtub. The look on her face was so seductive and the sudden grunt she made signaling me that I was all the way inside of her. I slowly pounded her flesh against the wall of the shower making certain that she felt every inch of me inside of her. The moans she made while digging her nails into my back made me start to slam into her with no mercy. I slipped out of her moistness only to have her get on her knees and take me into her mouth while the water ran down our bodies. I ran my fingers through her hair and grabbed the back of her head and pulled her closer as I began to cum. She slowed her pace and savored every drop of my liquid potion number nine. We made love once more before I left and it too was explosive. She had found a place on my friends list because of her willingness to please me although I was a mere stranger on his way to prison.

Jay offered me money to take to jail with me but I insisted that I was straight on cash. He wished me luck and told me that if everything goes right, he might be out of the country when I get out but I'll have a way to get in touch with him through Megan, who would be visiting me til my bid was over.

CHAPTER 29

NELLIS AIRFORCE BASE

Today is the day of my daughter's mother, Rissa's funeral. I must say it was one of the worst days of my life because my daughter took seeing her mother being put in the ground extremely hard, and although my sister-in-law offered her comfort to Isha, nothing would take the place of her mother. It was hard for me because I knew I was on my way to prison soon and could not be there for her or my new wife and kid.

After the funeral, I took advantage of what little time I had left by spending quality time with my son and daughter. I even got my son's mother to commit to making sure that she gets my daughter on the weekends so she could be with her brother.

My mother and I made up and almost fell out again when she tried to convince me that I should leave my daughter in Baltimore with her family until I get out of prison and can take care of her. I wanted my son and daughter with me in California so they could visit, but getting my son's mother to agree to letting my son go would take an act of God himself. I decided to leave Isha in Baltimore until Brishette had the baby, then I'd bring her out to California to start her new life with me and Brishette.

I tied up my loose ends, made sure everybody was organized before I turned myself in. I even flew to Jamaica and took care of Tywla. She agreed to take care of the house while I was gone and she would get money every month through Western Union. Twyla got all mushy and told me how she couldn't stop thinking about me and she pray everyday that one day, that I will love her like she loves me.

I was sent to Federal Prison at Nellis Airforce Base in Nevada. Of all the places, they send me to Sin City, home of the Bunny ranches. Just the thought of it was going to be torture.

Federal prison was very different from state prison. The food was better, recreation was better, the guards or C.O.'s treated you with a little more respect. Oh yeah, the Education Programs were much better. They had outside college instructors come in to teach college courses.

After about 3 weeks, I had gotten myself a routine. I ran in the mornings at 6:00a.m., came back, took a shower and got ready for the Drug Program, which was Monday, Wednesday and Fridays at 7:45a.m. I got off for lunch at 10:00a.m., went back from 12:00 til 3:30p.m. They counted at 4:00-4:15p.m. We were gone to dinner by 5:00p.m. I had the rest of the day to do me. I had the same schedule on Tuesdays and Thursdays, except Tuesdays, Thursdays and Saturdays, I worked as a clerk in Education.

I took all sorts of classes in the evenings called A.C.E. Classes that were taught by inmates. Banking and Finance was taught by a convicted former bank president. He taught us how to be approved for loans and what banks looked for and how to negotiate for lower interest rates. We even learned how to approach the bank for repossessed cars and foreclosed properties.

Everything seemed to go well until around fifth month when I had to do something I hadn't done in a long time, bust a dude in his head. They assigned each inmate a folding metal chair to use in the room or cubicle and to take to the T.V. rooms to watch T.V. So I'm sitting there watching something for an hour and a dude comes out of nowhere and changes the T.V. I tell him "Aye, I'm watching that."

He responds, "Not no more, not on this T.V."

"Hold up, you just gone disrespect me like that?"

This stupid mutha fucka turned his back on me. Why did he do that. I picked up the chair, got a good grip on the legs with both hands and tried to smash his whole face in. I hit him so hard that he and his chair fell backwards, hitting the floor. Then, just as I was about to finish him off, I heard somebody say, "It ain't worth it."

I turned to look at the young looking Italian guy and I'm glad he stopped me because seconds later, the C.O.'s were coming in deep, screaming get on the floor. They saw all the blood and the boy holding his face. They immediately asked him who did this to you and it looked like he pointed me right out.

The moment the guy started using his hand pointing at everybody, I realized that either he didn't know who actually hit him or he didn't want to say.

They locked us down and told us we would remain locked down until someone comes forth and tells them who did this. Within hours, the Italian shot caller had recruited a bunch of guys to drop notes on some guy they wanted to get rid of, saying that they all saw him assault the guy. Of course the Lieutenant and Captain believe their snitches over some guy saying he had nothing to do with it.

They put they guy in the segregated housing unit {SHU}, which saved me from being locked up, security raised and transferred to another prison.

I found out that the Italian guy, Richie Giatano, was the unit clerk who worked for the counselor for three and a half years and had access sometimes to other inmates' paperwork. This access allowed him to read my paperwork and know that I wasn't "HOT." This is the name they gave to snitches.

I later learned that Ritchie was a master manipulator. He had simply used that situation to get rid of a gambling bookie who was his competition and at the same time he did something for a stand-up guy, me, who now owed him a favor.

I could live with that, especially when I learned what he needed from me. On the weekends and even some week days some of our guys would sneak out of the camp into the woods that led to a field, which ended at the highway. The hotel was a half mile from the prison. Now I see why learning who was stand-up and who wasn't was so important. Repaying the favor was simple, so I gladly accepted. I was left with a cell phone in the T.V. Room where we could see the officers if they came to count early. Because of the distance they had to walk, we had time to make the call to let them know to get back and it was easy to say you were in another dorm even though they already checked that because of the way the prison was made.

After watching how they moved and hardly ever getting caught I decided to try it myself if I got caught after feeding my sex appetite, it would have been worth my while. Many inmates never even get to smell some pussy, let alone get to taste and get lost inside of some.

CHAPTER 31

AIN'T NOTHING WRONG WITH BEING RICH

It had been around eight months since I jumped up and down in some warm juicy pussy. I was long overdue and so was China. Damn, we shared so much passion and emotion as we made love. She had me moaning and some more shit when she turned me out on the love beads or pleasure beads, or whatever you called them.

It was the first time I came so violently and had multiple orgasms. I thought only women had those. China poured almond oil on my dick and sucked and licked it off like she was in a contest and winning would save her life. Her pussy was so tight like a sexy young virgin. I enjoyed every stroke, but hearing China scream out when she came really did it for me.

After the explosive sex, I checked my watch, I had 52 minutes to get back. During the next 40 minutes, China explained to me that her Chinese uncle would be in L.A. next week and he would be expecting to visit the mansions, see the girls and meet me.

"So how do you tell him about me being in jail?"

"I don't, I'll tell him that you couldn't be here, something very important came up and you had to go out of town."

"You think he'll go for that?"

"He doesn't have a choice and he's really here to see me and see how

I'm doing. My uncle is no fool he knows my independent spirit will be useful to him and the family. I think my uncles may feel bad that my mother died trying to get away from them treating her like a prisoner and they want to keep me close and rich."

China said a mouthful and had my attention.

"Ain't nothing wrong with being rich, but you're already rich China with wisdom, rich with beauty, and so damn sexy, you could be a sex Goddess."

We both laughed before I kissed her goodbye as she dropped me off at the field brush and sticker bushes winding up on the side of the building. I made it inside just in time for count and without incident. I was able to hide my scratches with long pants and long sleeves. After count, China and I spoke for almost two hours on the cell phone I purchased for $200 from Richie. We discussed how we could take the mansion parties and the girls to another level by rotating girls every 90 days to and from Asia through her uncle's Hong Kong based Travel Agency and Escort Service, which spawned from Russia, London and Japan to the United States.

This partnership could be lucrative for us, as well as her uncle. It would give our mansion parties more exotic flavor having new girls from all over the world.

This would really put us in the game with the mansion parties. Girls has always been and will always be the lure for men with money. Now, even women pay for pleasure

with and by other women. It's no secret that sex still sells across the planet. So, the more girls we have and the more variety we offer, the more money we will make. I just didn't trust her Chinese family members. The stories about their intense prejudice didn't help at all. To do this would be a roll of the dice.

CHAPTER 32

TWO WEEKS LATER

"DeJohn Patterson report to visitation," the PA system blared throughout the camp. I was already anticipating the visit and had just spoke to Brishette 20 minutes ago to make sure she and the baby were still coming so I was ready to go.

This was my first visit from Wifey. I told her not to visit until the baby was a few months older. So it was my first time I got to see my beautiful baby addition to the family. You could tell I was feeling like a million bucks right about now.

It was all over my face.

You could also tell by all the nosey looks everybody- male and female- was giving us, that they all thought Brishette and the baby was drop dead gorgeous. Brishette was killing em with the Forest green leather two -piece 'I-club' set and her black Christian Louboutin Cate boots. My baby boy had a matching green baby outfit on.

"Damn, you look good," I said whispering in her ear as I reached down to kiss her while she held the baby - who looked to be sleeping in her arms - probably from the long ride and the wait they had to go through.

"I miss you so much Dee." slightly reaching up to hug me, making sure the baby was secure in her lap.

I eased into the seat next to her only to look into her beautiful brown penetrating eyes. That was one of the features that had me hooked. But more than anything, it was her style. She was a natural beauty, no make up or accessories necessary. Just poise and grace like my grandmother used to say about Minnie Ripperton back in the day. She used to say, "Now that's poise and grace, listen to that girl sing."

"Look at you. Now I know why I married you Brishette."

"Why did you marry me Dee?"

"Because you are everything I want and need in a woman. You're smart, sexy, independent, and a hell of a mother. I've watched you interact with Isha, you're a natural." The girl on the other side of us sitting with her boyfriend must have heard me because she looked my way and smiled.

"I just wish you were here with me and the baby. Oh, and I talked to Isha for a long time the other day. She's looking forward to coming to stay with us."

"She wrote me a cute little letter telling me she has a puppy. I miss her too, but this little bit of time is gonna be over in no time."

"How many more months?"

"About four or five baby. This thing is almost over. Then I'll be at the half-way house for a few months and plus I'll be able to come home on a weekend pass and be with you and the kids."

Right after count, Richie came by my cubicle calling my name in his thick Italian accent that only a true Sicilian could utter. "Yo DeJohn," stepping into my cube with a wide grin. "You must been doing something major out there kid. You got your wife rolling in a new model Big-Boy 7 series Beamer. Everybody was talking about how she looked like a movie star in the visiting room."

"Naw, she had all of that when I met her. You ain't seen how I do it yet. Wait until next week. As a matter of fact, I should have some pictures coming tomorrow or Tuesday of my girls."

"Your girls? What da mean? Don't tell me you're a pimp?"

"Naw, I wouldn't say that, but I would say that I'm the master of ceremonies."

"The what? Wadda ya some fucking priest or something? Wadda u do weddings or something."

"You're a funny dude Richie. No, I'm in the mansion business. I fill the mansion with nothing but strippers and throw mansion parties on the weekends."

"You're kidding me right?"

"Naw, I'm serious, you'll see. I can show you better than I can tell you. As soon as I get the pictures I'll let you see em."

The next day, during mail call, Richie standing close by, saw the office hand me the thick huge large manila envelope and asked, "They must be pictures."

Ritchie seemed to be as anxious as I was as he followed me to the hallway away from the crowd of mail seekers. Getting mail was like getting a Grammy or an Oscar Award. If they called your name over and over again, you felt like a celebrity.

The look on Ritchie's face as he and I viewed the pictures assembly line style, look and pass, said it all. I had never seen so many exotic and pretty girls who were associated or soon to be associated with me, in my life.

There were beautiful Black, Asian, Indian, Puerto Rican, and White girls. Some fully clothed, and some with bathing suits. Richie was thoroughly impressed.

"So let me get this straight DeJohn, are you telling me that all these girls work for you?"

"They're independent contractors. They work with me. They provide a service that I would otherwise not be able to provide."

"Would these services include sex?" Richie asked with a curious look on his face, "Because if that's the case, we might be able to do some business. Maybe you turn me on to some of these girls and maybe I can turn you on to a few things. I got a few tricks too my friend. I can show you how to really make some money, but I gotta get my cut."

"Of course, I wouldn't have it any other way," I said opening the next set of pictures. I showed Richie pictures of the Bentley Maybach and the mansion. He thought it belonged to somebody else until I explained how I got my first one and expanded from there.

"DeJohn, I know a lot of people. I'm tellin you, you look out for me, I'm gonna look out for you. I really like these two girls," putting two pictures aside. The truth is I didn't know all the girls at the mansion because China was responsible for recruiting. She knows who's hot in the clubs, who is gonna be good for business, etc.... She's been around them all.

"Ritchie, I'm gonna find out whether these girls will come up to visit you, but I can tell you now, these girls like money and are probably expensive."

"Money is not one of my problems. If money could buy freedom and happiness, I'd be free as a bird and happy as Mother Theresa."

The following weekend the questions and doubts were put to rest when all the nosey inmates, looking out of the window overlooking the visitor's parking lot, saw China pull up and get out the Bentley Maybach; looking like a runway model from Milan.

When I walked into the visiting room and everyone saw that China was there to see me, my celebrity status was confirmed. In jail a lot of people sit around and lie about who they are and what they had on the street, but when you really have it going on out there, your visits, your mail, and your commissary account tells it all. You don't have to say a word. Speaking of a word, all I could say was "Damn China, what are you trying to do to me?"

"What Dee?"

In a whispered tone I had to ask, "Did you have to get oiled down to get into them jeans cause they fitting. Your sexy three fingered gap is crazy girl, you know I'm addicted."

We both smiled then briefly kissed. "You want anything from the machines Dee?"

"Not right now, maybe later. I wanna hear about what happened."

"First of all, did you get the pictures I sent you of the girls? I sent two packages. The first one was some of the girls in the house, the second was the girls my uncle wants us to see."

"I thought that might have been the case because the Asian girls were in the larger envelope. So what's the deal with your uncle? What did he have to say? Did he like the spot?"

"Of course, he was impressed to see his little niece running such an upscale operation. He said this really had potential."

"So what did you talk about? How would the rotation go?

"It wouldn't be a rotation with our girls because he said the American girls would be too expensive in Asia. I see what he was saying. It's like the Asians girls are used to getting far less than the American girls. They would not make a lot money off the American girls in Asia, so they would only send Asian girls to add variety to our girls.

You see, these girls being sent over from Asia are in Canada, Los Angeles, New York, and Philadelphia at massage parlors. That's where they usually work with their Momma-suns."

"So how long do these girls stay over here in this country?"

"Most times they stay 90 days on visitor visas. That visa can be extended to 6 months but that's it, then they go back and new girls replace them..." I cut her off.

"Wait a minute China, you still haven't told me how we're gonna make money off the girls and what do we have to put up?"

"We don't put up anything more than what we been doing. All their expenses are paid. My uncle receives all the money and 40% goes into their accounts. They keep a record of their account and they often send money home to their families back in Asia."

"You still haven't told me how we make money."

"First of all, the new exotic girls bring more business Dee. More business is more money. The girls are trained to provide services. Remember they are used to working in massage parlors."

"Wait! I don't understand how everybody makes money."

"Look, my uncle knows how much the girls usually make a night, that's all he expects, but the massage parlor doesn't have the clientele that we have, so we can get more money. That money will be our money. The usual money they would make, I think he said the girls make about 6-8 thousand per night. That would only be half or a third of what we would make. It's like getting a 50% commission for just giving them the chance to network with our clients. Dee, I can see this working, plus I got a surprise for you."

"What kind of surprise?"

"You'll see next weekend if the visiting form is approved. I filled out one of the extra ones you sent me. Hopefully, I'll be bringing someone with me next weekend."

"What are you up to China? How do you know I wanna see this person?"

"Oh, you'll want to see them, trust me. I f I know you like I think I do, you'll enjoy this visit."

"If you say so. So what's going on with Splizzy? Why didn't he come up here?"

"He flew back to Baltimore for some show. He said something about the rapper Fabulous and his people wanted to meet him and they have been paying for studio time for Fabulous' cousin in Baltimore. He left this morning. He said to tell you to call him on his cell. Oh yeah, Steph told me to tell you to call him and send him a visiting form so he can come see you."

CHAPTER 33

PERSONAL ASSISTANT

China and I talked about everything from the night we first met to the threesome we had with Twyla. Damn, how could I forget that. One of my dreams finally came true.

China had just began to tell me how she's never had anybody to care about her like I did, then we walked out on the patio and took a few pictures. As we returned back to our seats, I heard someone call my name. China and I both turned to see who it was.

The nosey visitors who seemed to have been watching me and China like we were the Young and Restless now had a look on their faces like, "Oh shit." As she walked closer to where we sitting China asked the obvious, "Dee who is that?"

I stood up and greeted Megan, making sure not to put too much on it or to make China jealous. "Hey, what's going on Megan? Here....." I moved China's coat from the chair next to me so Megan could sit on the left side of me because there was no other seat across from or near us, aside from the seat that held China's coat and see through plastic purse which carried the many quarters we used on vending, her California Drivers license , and the Bentley Maybach keys.

"Hi, how are you doing DeJohn? Jay sent me to check on you, so who is your friend?"

"That's the magnificent China Doll. China, this is Megan. She's a friend of the guy you met at the Holiday Inn's brother. Remember? Before I went in?"

"Oh yeah, how are you doing?" I could tell China wasn't feeling this intrusion, especially where I totally forgot to tell her about Megan and that my man Jay was gonna be sending her to visit when he wanted to get messages to me.

Megan helped a little by apologizing, "I apologize for the interruption. There's no way I could have called. It all happened so suddenly. When I got home last night, I had a message to go see DeJohn. I don't know if you knew this, but I'm like his personal assistant. I get paid to handle his affairs."

"So, what's up? You can talk in front of China. She's my partner in crime."

"Well, he just wanted me to tell you something about some guy name Splizzy...."

"What about Splizzy?" I said becoming very curious because I never mentioned Splizzy to Jay, so how could he know Splizzy?

"He just wanted me to tell you that this Splizzy guy knows about what happened to your daughter's mother, and that the people that he thinks are his friends are not; so he needs to watch his back."

"Wait, wait, say that again, he knows something about my daughter's mother? And what people is he talking about?"

"Hold up, so when are you gonna talk to Jay again? I need to talk to him or you need to get some more information."

"Oh wait, he did say something else. He told me to tell you to holler at Step....." I cut her off.

"Step? Who......do you mean Steph?"

"Stef, Step, something like that. He said that you need to get with him because he knows the people."

"What people? What people is he talking about?"

"I don't know DeJohn. I'm just delivering the message, don't kill the messenger."

This shit is crazy. What the fuck is going on? What is Jay talking about and I know he knows Steph, but how does he know about Splizzy and what does Splizzy know about Rissa's murder and why didn't he tell me? Is that why he didn't come to see me? All this shit was running through my head. My appetite was gone, my mind racing with 'what if's'. "So when are you gonna talk to him again?"

"I'll probably hear from him tonight because he's gonna wanna know what happened today and did I make it to see you."

"Megan, when am I gonna hear from you again? When are you

coming back up here? Better yet, is the number you gave me still a good number?"

"That was my cell phone number, that number is still good. You can call me whenever."

"Alright, I'll call you tonight. I got your number in my book."

"Oh, it was nice meeting you China."

"You too," China responded.

Megan left, leaving China and I to talk about her mind-blowing message from Jay. I could tell China was just as confused and bewildered as I was. What was Jay talking about? What did Splizzy know about Rissa's murder and why did he mention that Steph knew the people. After hearing that, my appetite was gone, my mind was off and wandering and I couldn't wait to get back to get the day over with. It was killing me to know I had to wait until after the 4p.m. Stand-up count for all the administrative staff to leave the prison because that's when everybody goes out into the woods digging up their cell phones or in my case cell phone in a jar. Usually there was a few guys who get paid to keep people's cell phones in the prison. You turn to them after seeing other people either get caught or after a major shake-down where they move all the inmates to an isolated area, search em if necessary, then the whole prison's staff, women and all, tear the inmates housing quarters up trying to find contraband.

When they were done, you could hear guys complaining for days and sometimes writing grievances about the way the searching officers disrespected their rooms. Stuff all over the floor. Your living area was "raped" as we called it.

So after that, the "stash boys" came in real handy. You paid them a monthly or weekly fee to safely hide your cell phone because losing them to a shake-down could be expensive because if you didn't get it through visitation, then you or somebody else got it by running through the woods to get a bag. They had a guy who did that too. These inmates were about their paper too. Some charge as little as $50.00 to grab a small bag for you but the others might charge $200-$300. In those duffle bags would sometimes be cell phones for sale. These guys would buy pre-paid cell phones with minutes and sell them for as much as $400.00. So, $30.00 - $40.00 per month was a blessing to pay for a guy to keep and hide your phone.

Just as it was getting ready to get dark, my stash man came through with my T-mobile pre-paid phone with the black car piece. I checked my battery power and I had four out of five bars, so I was good to go. I put the phone's ear piece in my right ear and one of my Sony walkman's ear buds in the left ear letting the other one hang inside my T-shirt. I ran the wires down into my shirt so all you could see was the wires going into my shirt. The two tone ear bud and the hands free ear piece was not a perfect match, but they both were black so as long as I don't let nobody get too close I was good.

CHAPTER 34

SET THE WHOLE THING UP

I already had on the athletic supporter jock strap. I used it to stick my phone down in my dip and put my radio on my waist or hold it in my hand so it looked like I was listening to the radio but the radio was far from being on.

A lot of people got caught because they keep taking their phone out to make multiple calls to different people, but I only called one person, who called everybody else on the three-way.

I made my call and waited for an answer. China had made it back safely and was now in personal assistant/secretary mode. I stuck the phone in my Jock strap, put on a skull cap to hide the mismatched earpieces, then headed for the prison walking track.

I walked pass several inmates who I had to speak to or they would be wondering what was up. So I acted like I was singing a rap on the radio and bobbing my head to a non-existing beat while I listened to and responded to China until I got on the track then I had her dial Steph. He answered on the third ring.

"Hello," Steph yelled over the extremely loud background noise. "What's good?"

"Dee? Wait...wait. I can hardly hear you."

"Yeah, it's loud as shit. Where you at?"

"I'm on the studio lot at Paramount. Let me try to find a quiet spot around here somewhere. So what's good? How you get to call me without calling collect?"

"I got China on here, she hooked me...."

"Hey Kareem."

"Oh hey China, how are you?"

"I'm good, where my girl at?"

"She's in Cancun with her mother and little sister for her Mother's birthday."

"Oh yeah, she did tell me about that."

"So what's up Dee?"

"I need to find out what's going on with that situation with my daughter's mother."

"Yeah, I been told you to get at me."

"You didn't tell me to get at you about that."

"Can you call me back tonight?"

"I don't know, but I'll try. I'm on a cell phone right now and I don't know if I'll be able to use it later on."

"Yeah, well now ain't the time. I can't talk right now, but I heard a little something about that situation and that ain't something we need to be talking about on the phone. I need to come up there and see you anyway and we can talk then."

"I'm a have to send you a visiting form. You fill it out and send it back then they add you to my visiting list because it ain't like the state where anybody can come see you as long as they got I.D. In the Feds, you have to be on an approved visiting list, so send it right back when you get it, awight?"

"Awight, I'll do that and try to call me back anyway. I gotta get back before the start tripping."

All of this indirect information was starting to take its toll, first Megan telling me that Jay sent her to tell me about Splizzy knowing something about the murder, then Steph saying he knows something, but I'm the last to know. I wonder is this how they treat people who're not from L.A. Why am I the last to find out what really happened to my daughter's mother?

Over the next couple of months, I had sent out several visiting forms and the visits became more and more interesting. Steph finally made it up to see me. I was numb when he left.

Finding out that Splizzy had my daughter's mother killed and how my daughter was never really kidnapped because it was just a plot to get me to pay for the contract on my daughter's mother. Splizzy set the whole thing up when he found out that Rissa was starting to work for the police.

I felt responsible because I told him to watch her and if I hadn't told Splizzy that, then he might not have found out that she was working with the police. Then maybe we'd all be in Prison for conspiracy to commit murder. Now I feel like there's a side of me that wants to kill Splizzy but another side of me wants to thank him for saving us.

Then being in jail, although I only have a few more months before I graduate the drug program and get the year off and six months halfway house, makes me feel like a sitting duck for the Feds. What if they are investigating her murder? What if somebody talks?

Steph says that Splizzy needs to lay low for a while because rumor has it that the Latino gang may try to come at Splizzy to get rid of the only other link to them because now that Rissa is gone, there's only Splizzy left and he knows about both murders. Rissa and her undercover police boyfriend from Baltimore. Maybe that's why Splizzy went back to Baltimore and ain't come to see me like he said.

Tonight was the night. Ritchie set up a meeting with the hacker -boy that he bragged about for months. Ritchie was not dumb by a long shot. In a way, he was a lot like myself, always pooling his resources. As soon as Ritchie learned that I had a gang of girls working with me who danced for money, he saw an opportunity to get a lot of money while he was in jail. Ritchie made a deal with me that if he hooked me up with this hacker -boy Josh, I would in exchange, give him a percentage of the action which would be several thousand dollars. Affording him enough to live comfortably through out the entire five and a half years Ritchie had to go before he would be released.

As an extra bonus, I had to throw in a couple of girls for Ritchie and Josh after the meeting. China brought two girls who were game and ready for whatever. I could tell by their names "Satin" and "Creamy" that they were gonna be something else.

There was just something about tonight that didn't feel right I had been having this uneasy feeling all day but against my better judgment, I decided to go anyway. Besides, I couldn't just not show up. Not when so much was at stake.

CHAPTER 35

THE WESTERN UNION MEETING

"Yo Dee, are you ready? Everybody is in place. Sabatino is going to go with us to the highway and bring back the bag. So he's gonna turn around and come back and you and I are going to jump in the car. Where's your gloves?"
"They are in my pocket."
"Aright, let's do this and get back."
It was now 10:40p.m. After the routine 10:00p.m. Count. We left out the side door near the T.V. Room crouched low and made our way swiftly into the woods. I had never been this nervous before. It just didn't feel right. We all made it to the highway where we spotted China driving slow in the opposite direction. I directed her from the cell phone to our location. As she pulled up I opened the back door and pulled the black Glad trash bag from the back seat. The bag was filled with everything from Black and Milds to bottles of flavored Bacardi, not to mention the candy, cookies, shrimp, and wife beaters in the bag. Once Sabatino got the bag China pulled off.
"Make sure nobody is following us," I managed to get out despite my being out of breath from all the running through those woods.
"We're good. No one is behind us. I got two rooms next to each other

like you asked. The girls are in one room and we're gonna be in the other for the meeting."

Damn, China was so calculated. So sharp, all I had to do was give her the play and she was all over it. It's hard to find guys on point like that let alone a woman.

"Do the rooms have connecting......"

"Keep your heads down, there's lights behind me. Should I keep going pass the hotel or pull in because I'm almost there?"

"Keep going pass it and then do a U-turn to find out whether they are following you." Ritchie spoke for the first time since we got into the car.

"I'm gonna pull into this Dairy Queen parking lot and turn around." China said sounding like she was on some illegal caper or something.

"What's the car behind you doing?" Ritchie asked.

"They turned off."

We made it safely to the hotel. The girls did who knows what to Ritchie in the adjacent room while Josh, China, and I had our meeting. In a way, it didn't seem like I was in jail. It was more like I was at home already having a clandestine meeting at a hotel, but the reality set in when we heard a knock at the door.

I had heard stories about inmates getting caught red handed at the hotel after the hotel manager called the prison to report that he'd seen some guys in prison clothing but that was not the case with us because we shed the prison garb over top our gray sweats when we got in the car. We were wearing gray when we got out. So what could this be about. So, I quickly went into the bathroom and hid behind the door while China answered the door. Josh remained seated at the table by the window.

"Who is it?" China screamed through the door.

"I think you left your lights on in your car," the female voice beyond the door blurted out.

That was not good at all because if the lights were left on then they could have possibly seen the prison greens on the floor of the back seat. But I don't recall the light being on when we walked away from the car.

"Thank you," China screamed back through the door. Josh went to the window as I came out of the bathroom. "Damn, that's not your car, that's my car. I'll be right back. Let me turn the light out."

I thought to myself as Josh left, that's all we need is to get the wrong attention. Any mistakes could be fatal in our situation.

Josh returned and I told him straight up that we needed to get this meeting underway, so that we can get back. "We don't have a lot of time. So, explain to us how this is supposed to work."

Josh was a young white kid somewhere in his mid to late twenties. He was about six feet tall with reddish sandy hair and medium build. You know, the baseball cap, t-shirt, jeans and sketchers sneaker type. "Okay, I don't know what Ritchie has already told you, but it's not that complicated to understand it. The complicated part is doing it and you let me handle all of that. First of all, you'll need to have girls with heart. You will need to make them understand that this is perfectly legal during the time of the transactions because they are very few ways that the cardholders or the Western Union representatives could know that these transactions are fraudulent. There's just no way except that the cardholders have a fraud alert on their account. Then the credit card company may call the cardholder......"

"So how can the girls know that?" China asked Josh.

"Look, I've been doing this for a long time and it is so simple once everything is set up properly. So you really don't have to worry about that and remember they're not going into the bank to pick up, only supermarkets and drug stores. But to answer your question, they won't but again, there's a small chance, if any of getting caught."

"I still don't understand how you do it. I thought Western Union has to call you back. I know about the part where you can manipulate the caller I.D. To show whatever number you want. Ritchie kind of explained that part........"

Josh cut me off, "look, it's simple. I used to be a security specialist for Pacific Bell telephone company. In other words, I was the company's hacker in charge of preventing infiltration into the company's main server and secure data bases. Look, this may sound a little cocky, but I'm probably in the top five hackers in the country. I know my shit and I don't usually deal with people I don't know, but I've been dealing with Ritchie since we were knee-high in grade school. He's my best friend. So, I'm not doing this for you, I'm doing it for him. So let me make this clear. I don't want to meet anybody, I don't want to see anybody and we will communicate over an encrypted line. Look, there's a program called Zfone which lets you place encrypted calls between two computers. You're gonna need a microphone and an earphone headset. You can get them from Radio Shack.

"You still haven't said how this is gonna work."

"Look, like I said, it's simple. We're gonna start with increments of $2500.00 because that's not over $30000.00 which is the suspicion threshold for Western Union. They start getting all crazy when you go over $3000.00 so we stay under it. Now, there will be ten girls. Each can do a minimum of two transactions per day at $2500.00. That's $5000.00 times ten is $50,000.00 a day. This first time we will do a three day run to see how it turns out if everything goes well. Then we will do more. That's $150,000.00. Ritchie gets 5%, which is $7500.00, the rest we split 60/40. You guys get 60 because it's your responsibility to pay the girls. Like I said, I don't meet anybody. You will be given instructions on depositing my money into an account. My cut is $57,000.00, your cut is $85, 500.00.

China seemed irritated, "You still haven't told us how this works, you've told us what we need to do but you haven't explained how you're gonna pull this off and how we're not just walking into a trap."

"Look, I don't have to explain anything to you."

I couldn't let him get away with that. " Hold up playboy, let me explain something to you. These girls you'll be dealing with are not crack heads, some of them make thousands every night. So they are not expendable. In fact, they are quite valuable and we've been doing fine without you. Like you said , you're doing this for Ritchie, we're doing it to make money. So, if you can't convince us that this is something that can work, we're wasting each others time and I could be laid up with the most beautiful girl in the world right now." I gave a quick look at China and then returned my eye to eye contact with Josh, offering a slight smirk.

Josh begrudgingly complied, at that point I knew he needed us just as much as we needed him. Shit he was talking numbers like I've done on the mansion parties. $150,000.00 in three days, so I was all ears.

"Okay look, I have access to financial profiles. You know, bank accounts and credit card information. Dates of birth, social security numbers and all of that. Everything the bank requires. So I have thousands of credit card account numbers with matching address and telephone numbers. I can call Western Union with a voice changer and be male or female. The problem most people have is Western Union requires you call from your home phone, so your number shows on their caller I.D. then as an extra step of security they want to call you back.

"That's the part I've been trying to get you to explain so we can end this meeting and you can enjoy yourself with the girls who are probably wondering what's taking you so long," China said to Josh with her sinister million dollar smile. I couldn't wait to get my hands on China because we were running out of time. We had to be back soon.

"Well, that's where I come in. I can hack into the telephone company's server and route a customer's calls to any number I want. So, if Western Union calls the card holder's number, it will ring on my pre-paid cell phone."

"Yeah, we got that, but what about the caller I.D.?"

"That's the easy part. I have a program that allows me to program any number I want into the outgoing line, which I would program the cardholders number and it would appear that I'm calling from the card holder's home number. Look, trust me, I know my shit. If you ave got a lot of girls, like Ritchie says, then we can make millions and fast. They just have to be willing to travel. So that's really all you need. Here's my cell phone number, call when you're ready, that means when you get the microphone and earphone pieces. Call me so we can get you set up on the Zfone.

"You'll be dealing directly with China until I get out. When you've got to get a message to me you contact China on the secure line. I'll be in touch with her all the time. So we have a deal, I think this could be the beginning of something big."

"You betcha," Josh extended his hand. China and I both shook hands with Josh. "It was a pleasure meeting you both."

"Yeah, you too, now go and enjoy yourself and tell Ritchie to be ready in 30 minutes. I hope you can handle two girls at once because once Ritchie leaves you'll have both girls to yourself until I get back from dropping Dee and Ritchie off. Oh, and don't play too rough with the girls."

"I promise, I won't." Josh smiled and left to join his friend Ritchie being entertained by Creamy and Satin.

CHAPTER 36

WE GOTTA GET BACK NOW

"China, we have to stop meeting like this." I said jokingly to China as I pushed her on the bed. "You gone get me in trouble, you know I'm a married man."

"Ain't nobody tell you to go and get married. I never figured you to be the marrying type, but I guess I was wrong."

As I laid on top of China looking in her eyes about to kiss her juicy lips and just thinking about how good it would feel to slide into her like home base in the bottom of the ninth with a tied score in the World Series, China busted my bubble.

"You might as well not even get started cause you ain't getting none."

"Aw man, don't do that China. I'm hard as penitentiary steel and you got the cure between your legs and I risked five more years in jail to get some of your goodies....."

"No, you risked five more years to meet with Josh about making money because that's all you think about."

"What? I can't believe you said that." I was moving to get off of her, feeling some type of way.

"I'm just kidding. I know you thought you were gonna get some but the fact of the matter is, I'm on my period. Unless you're into bloody marys, plus we don't have time."

I got off the bed and turned towards the bathroom and China stopped me. "Awww, look at you. You look like you just lost your best friend. Cum-----meere poor baby, I know what you need." Reaching over and grabbing my sweat pants pulling them down just enough to allow my pokey man out to stand attention. Just as she grabbed it ever so seductively and leaned down to take it in her mouth, a loud bang on the door made me grab my sweatpants and pull them up and again retreated behind the bathroom door.

"Who is it? China screamed.

The banging became louder and more consistent, nothing like the soft knocks earlier when someone alerted us that Josh's car lights were on. This sounded like the police for sure. Something told me not to go but I went against my better judgment. Damn, if I get caught, I throw away a whole year and a half because I get kicked out of the Drug Program. So instead of getting out in a few months after finishing up the program, I'd have two more years plus any new time that they might give me for escape. All sorts of things were going through my mind like knocking one of them down and making a run for the woods and try to get back before they did or telling them that my life was in danger in the prison but what would be my excuse for being in a hotel room with a beautiful girl like China.

Anyway, China peeped out of the curtain and saw that it was Ritchie but why was he banging like he was crazy? China opened the door.

"Where Dee at? We gotta get back."

I walked out of the bathroom, "What's wrong?"

"We got problems. Sabatino just called my cell. He said some dudes just jumped a guy in the bathroom. They hit the guy with locks-n-socks and they say he's bleeding pretty bad from his head. That means they are gonna rush him to the hospital and wake up everybody and make everybody take off their shirts and show their hands and shit. That means we gotta get back now. I don't know if we'll make it back in time to make the count or what but we need to get outta here now!"

"Let me grab my purse and tell the girls I'll be right back."

"China, they'll be fine until you get back. We gotta go now."

It seemed like as soon as we were all standing around the car waiting for China to get in and unlock the doors, a State Trooper rode by glancing over at us. A white guy, a black guy and a Chinese girl in the middle of the night at a hotel across from the prison on a non-visiting Wednesday night.

"Hurry up, he's turning around. Just act normal," I said in a hurried voice. We got into the car and was just about to pull out when the officer pulled into the hotel's parking lot. "Oh shit! China don't go by him, go out the other way." China backed out of the spot and turned to the right heading towards the trooper. "What are you doing?" I asked kicking the prison clothes under the back seat.

"I got this, let me handle him." She pulled a short distance from his car and asked the officer. "Excuse me sir, could you please tell me where an all night diner is close by?"

The trooper gave a suspicious but friendly smile and said, "Well that all depends on what kind of food you like because if you go south there's a Denny's about five or six miles from here, to the north there's a diner just above the interchange. I recommend the Denny's myself because the other one is a bit further unless you don't mind the trip." He looked right over at me in my sweats, then glanced at Ritchie in the back. China flashed her million dollar smile disarming the trooper. "Thank you so much officer." She pulled off making sure to turn on blinkers and all even though there was no traffic at this time of the night. But we were hardly out of the woods. The officer pulled out right behind us! "He's right behind us, so I can't stop to let you guys out. I'm gonna have to keep going. Wait, there's a gas station up ahead. I'm gonna pull in and start to get out, let him go by then I'll go back." China threw her blinker on and made the left turn into the gas station which looked deserted. The attendant was probably asleep. I didn't want to turn around even in the passenger seat. China pulled back out of the gas station and made the right back towards our jump out spot. It seemed like as soon as the state trooper saw us pull out he got behind us again. Then he suddenly turned on his lights and siren, whoop, whoop. I thought this can't be happening. I'm contemplating jumping out and making a run for the woods. "China pull over, wait until he gets out and pull off and let us out and keep going until you get back to the hotel. Fuck em, cause we gotta get out of here."

China pulled over and the trooper sped by us. Damn, that was a close call. Time was running out for us real fast. China dropped us at the drop spot and we hauled ass through them woods. We came up on the side door, it was locked. "Shit come on Dee, we gotta make it to the other door."

"Damn, what are you gonna tell em?"

"Once we get inside, we split up. Stop at the first person's cubicle you know and get rid of your shoes and take off your sweat shirt so you have just your T-shirt, sweatpants, and shower shoes. Damn, you're sweating like a muther fucker." Ritchie said to me as the beads of sweat poured down my face like I've been working out for an hour. We got in the building, all the lights were on. It was no way we weren't gonna get caught. The side hall was clear but we heard the correction officer's talking, so we knew they were close by. I managed to get to the second cubicle from the hallway to a French guy named Sanjay who was in the drug class with me. I could trust him cause I've seen him make moves before. I took off my sweat shirt and boots. He lent me his shower shoes and some toilet paper to wipe the sweat from my forehead.

I hurried back into the hallway and walked quickly towards my cubicle which was past the bathroom and a connecting hallway. Just when I thought I made it I heard the officer call me.

"Hey, what are you doing out here in the hallway, everyone was told to stay in their cubicles until further notice. Where do you sleep?"

"In my cubicle right there."

"Right where?"

"By the bathroom in F dorm."

"F dorm? Then what are you doing up here in C-dorm?"

"I was in my friend's cubicle talking cause he go home tomorrow ."

"Have a seat on the bench right there, and don't move."

I sat on the bench in the hall, Ritchie had gotten away, but I got caught. Damn, I was so close. If only I had made it a little further. I could see into D dorm, everyone was standing. The officers were making everybody take their shirts off and reaching out their hands. I know they were probably thinking I must have had something to do with the fight in the bathroom. Within minutes the lieutenant came out into the hallway.

"Why is he out here, what did he do?"

I quickly spoke up, "I didn't do nothing, I did what the officer said to do. They told us to stay in your cubicle until further notice. I was in somebody else's cubicle and I didn't want to go out there while all this confusion was going on. I didn't want you to think I was involved in what happened."

"What do you know about what happened?" the lieutenant asked.

"I don't know anything except somebody got beat up in the bathroom and there was a lot of blood."

The officer interrupted, "Stand up and take your shirt off." I took off my T-shirt, "Now turn around," I turned around. "Hold your hands out, okay put your shirt back on. "What do you want me to do with him lieutenant?"

"Go to your dorm and don't let me catch you in this hallway again." I quickly went back to my dorm. GOD was definitely with me this night.

CHAPTER 37

TEST RUN

Two weeks went by without incident. I stayed low key and out of the way just in case they suspected or somebody told that I was leaving out.

China surprised me with a special visit; which confirmed something for me, like China would be good for recruiting other women who were bisexual. I couldn't believe it when I walked out into the visiting room. There was China looking all good as usual and had the young cutie from Jamaica, Twyla, with her.

"What a surprise, how did you pull this off China?" I said before I hugged and kissed China then turned to Twyla, who was smelling like some cotton candy or something good to eat. I went to hug Twyla intending to kiss her on her cheek, but she turned to kiss me in the mouth.

"Damn, this is really a surprise. So how long have you been in the states Twyla and is everything okay with the house?"

"I've been here only two days and everything is fine with the 'ouse. Mr. Myles came by and put an alarm on the 'ouse. China has been showing me around. She is so nice Mr. Dee."

"I bet she is," I said smiling at China because I know China probably got this young girl turned out and in love. I can just imagine what a woman can make another woman feel by knowing her body. I always wanted to get lessons from a lesbian on how to master the art of pleasing a woman. China broke my chain of thought.

"Dee, I gotta fill you in on what's been going on. Even Twyla made some money yesterday and I took her shopping to get an outfit so she could look pretty for you today."

"Damn, that thing with Josh must be sweet. So, where we at on that anyway? What kind of numbers did you do with Josh?" I asked wanting to know the extent of the business done with Josh.

"We did a test run in Nevada at the Casinos. He just wanted to see how ready the girls were. We only used ten girls for that one. At $2500.00 each and they went three days in a row. So that's $150,000.00, so we know it works like a charm but Josh said we got to hit them hard and fast and get out."

"So what is he talking about?"

"He wants us to get as many girls together as we can so we can do one big run and stop because Western Union will catch on but if we get it all done quick, by the time they find out what is going on, we'll be long gone and they'll be out of millions." China said with a sinister grin on her face. "Plus, I called my Uncle in Hong Kong and told him I need to talk with him on urgent and lucrative business. He sent someone to pick me up and took me to some restaurant where we talked and he called me back yesterday and told me my uncle said it's a go, he will supply all the girls we need. They explained that they have at least ten massage parlors in each city and at least fifteen girls in each house, so that's one hundred and fifty girls in each city."

"Damn, your uncle is doing it China."

"You should've heard him tell me how they train Asian and Russian girls to never talk if they ever get caught because they still have access to their families in China and Russia and that some of the girls are at the end of their stay so they can be used to get some money real fast before they leave this country. He also told me that when the girls are on their periods, this transaction would be great for them because they can still earn money for their families back in China and Russia."

"So, how many girls is Josh talking about?"

"Dee, we talking about doing it big and being done with it. So we're looking at ten cities in Florida and ten cities in California. My uncle is gonna produce most of the girls because we only have about forty girls. So that's three hundred and sixty girls in two states or eighteen cities."

"Hold up China."Twyla came back over with the hot wings.

"What kind of drink do you want? Water or soda? I hope your wings are hot enough for you Mr. Dee."

"Twyla, just get me a water. I don't drink sodas."

"What about you China? What do you want me to get you?"

"I'll take a pepsi Twyla, thank you."

"Okay, I'll be right back."

I couldn't wait to finish hearing what China had up her sleeve. "so let me make sure I heard you right. You're saying that ya'll getting ready to do twenty cities in two different states and your uncle is supplying three hundred and sixty girls. China that's a lot of girls. Ya'll sure this ain't too big for ya'll to pull off?"

"Dee, it's really kind of simple. Look, two girls will be chosen from each of my uncle's ten massage parlors in each city. That's twenty girls in each city. He's gonna do eighteen cities like it ain't nothing and we are gonna do the other two cities with our forty girls. The hardest part is getting all the I.D.'s together and Josh says that's what he does. He said he's been living for this moment. He said that's why he doesn't mess with a lot of people because it's just not worth his time and the people think too small."

"Shiiit, that's crazy numbers this kid is talking about. China do ya'll realize how big this is? We'll talk later, Twyla is on her way back over here."

"Dee we looking at four hundred girls at an average of $4000.00 each because we can't do em all for $ 2500.00 even, so some are gonna be $21, 22, 23, 24, you know mix it up but it will average out to about $4,000.00 each...."

I cut her off, "I said we'll talk later. Thank you Twyla. Why didn't you get yourself something."

"I'm not really hungry because we ate on the way 'ere when we stopped for gas, plus I've been eating peppermints." I loved to hear her Jamaican accent, it was a real turn on.

We all took a picture together before the C.O. ended the visit. After the visitors left, I couldn't help but think about the crazy numbers that China was talking about.

CHAPTER 38

DON'T CAUSE US TO BECOME ENEMIES

Just after count, Ritchie came to get me to walk the track and talk. He was beyond ecstatic when I explained to him that Josh and China was planning something large that might be worth about five million and if it happens, he could be looking at around two to two hundred and fifty thousand.

"Stop breaking my fucking balls Dee. Are you serious? Oh shit!" The look on my face showed that I was dead serious. "You're fucking serious aren't you. I told you this fucking kid Josh is a freaking genius. Every since we were kids he was always smarter than everybody in the neighborhood."

"Hold up Ritchie, don't get your hopes up just yet because it hasn't happened yet. They have to coordinate 400 girls to strike twice a day for three days in a row."

"Dee, I told you this kid was a gold mine. I'm still trying to figure out how I'm gonna spend the $7500.00 I'm getting off the first job and these guys are planning to sting em for meal tickets. This is too good to be true DeJohn."

"You might have to take a smaller cut because there are so many more people to take care of...." I fore-warned him.

Ritchie interrupted, "How much smaller are we talking here?"

"I'm not saying it's gonna happen, but it could happen but it probably won't be no less than 3%, but that is still one hundred forty-four thousand. So you still come off like a thief in the night. You're just sitting back and collecting. You can't beat that."

"We're gonna have to make some arrangements because I can't have all that money on my prison account, but don't know who I could trust with all that dough. My uncle Vito has a construction company that makes a couple million a year but he's a slimy low life....."

"Ritchie you need to start thinking investments and trusts. I can hook you up with a lawyer to set up a trust for your kids or your family that will have a trustee that makes investments that make your money grow or you can put the money in a numbered account in Panama or Singapore. They have safe-havens just like the Swiss Banks and right now there are no agreements with the U.S. So your privacy is safe there, plus you'll have a international debit card that you can use like a credit and ATM card."

Ritchie and I talked for over an hour about what to do with all the money we were about to make and how no one would have ever guessed that you could be pulling this kind of thing off while you're in prison. When I returned back to the unit, the guy went and got my cell phone from the stash spot outside in the woods. I checked my voice messages only to find that Brishette and Splizzy had called.

I called Brishette first to make sure the baby was okay. She answered on the 3rd ring.

"Hello DeJohn...."

"How did you know it was me?"

"Oh yeah, I forgot about the caller I.D. I don't know where my mind was just now. So what's going on? How's the baby?"

"The baby is fine. Speaking of the baby, we really need to talk because I just got some disturbing news from my sister's best friend Marci who works at the hospital where you apparently got arrested. Obviously, this girl you've been seeing has a big mouth and can't keep her business to herself....."

Aww shit I said to myself, here comes the bullshit.

"So please enlighten me on how you have two children being born so close in time without you cheating on me and please don't try to deny that it is your baby by this girl Candice. That is her name right?"

"Look Brishh..."

"Don't Brishhh me, just answer me DeJohn because I am really upset right now and I promise you that you don't need me to be your enemy because I go above and beyond revenge...."

"Hold on somebody is coming." I put the phone under my pillow while the officer went by after scaring the shit out of me. I had a funny feeling that this was not going to be my night.

After the officer left our dorm, I returned to my call, "I'm back....hello?"

"What, Dee how could you do this to me? I trusted my heart body and soul to you and you crossed me....."

"Stop right there, first of all, maybe you have forgotten but I am your husband. I married you because I love you and I want to spend the rest of my life with you. This is not a game of hearts. This shit is real and just so you know, that was something that happened when I first got here and needed a place to stay, I was renting a room from Candice and one night I had too much to drink and one thing led to another. I didn't even know she was pregnant. She kept it from me because she was planning to get an abortion because she knew I would not want a baby..." Brishette sniffles became a little less frequent indicating that maybe I was getting through to her.

"So why didn't you tell me about her?"

"Are you out of your mind? And risk losing you over somebody that I don't even hardly know or care about? Like I said, this was not a relationship, it just happened that night. There is nothing serious between us, but I did promise her that I'd take care of my child. I'm going to do that no matter what the circumstances."

"DeJohn, I'm not gonna let you hurt me and get away with it."

"I would never hurt you Brishette, not intentionally. As I said, I married you because I believe we were made for each other."

"How do I know you're not lying to me right now?"

"You know! Follow your heart, whatever it tells you, run with it because you're not gonna be able to say that I don't love you and I'll be home in a couple of more months and you'll see for yourself. I'm sorry that this happened and that I didn't come to you as soon as I knew but there was just too much going on. I couldn't risk losing you. You're too important to me."

"DeJohn, the baby is crying, you want to hold on or you just want to call me back?"

"I'm going to call you back baby because they are getting ready to count soon and this phone needs charging because there's not much juice left on the battery, plus I need to see you. You need to come up here and see me this weekend coming up. I need to see and talk to you in person, so when are you coming?"

"DeJohn I need you to understand that I am not the average girl who's heart you can play with and get away with it. I'd rather us get a divorce now if you can't be true to this relationship because I'm really not the one. Please don't cause us to become enemies. I'm begging you please."

More and more she started sounding like a deranged and badly wounded woman who wold do anything to get back at you if you hurt her. "what the hell have I gotten myself into," I thought to myself. I don't know if my calming words were even making a difference, but I continued anyway. "Brishette, I know you are probably second guessing my love for you, but I can assure you that if you look at my past record, you'll see that I am a man of my word and when I say something, I mean it."

"DeJohn, I'm not saying that you don't love me, that's not what I'm saying. I just don't want you to end up like the others....."

"What's that suppose to mean? Like the others, like what others? What are you talking about Brishette?"

"DeJohn, I gotta go. I have to change the baby and get the bottles ready. Plus I'm sleepy baby. DeJohn just promise you won't hurt me because I swear I can't take another betrayal."

"Stop worrying all the time. You worry too much. You need to relax a little because I ain't going nowhere. I'm all yours. Stop worrying. Didn't I come back from Baltimore when I went to my cousin Stevie's funeral? Didn't I marry you like I promised? Didn't I stop selling drugs like I said?"

"Yes," she said with a hint of defeat in her voice.

"Then why do you keep worrying? Why you don't trust me? You need to think about that and let me know when I call you back."

"Okay, I love you DeJohn."

"I love you too baby, now go handle your business and I'll call as soon as I can."

It seemed like all the pretty girls are crazy as hell. Like Halle Berry, Robin Givens, Naomi Campbell, not to mention Monica and Left Eye(rest in peace!). In their world, they are just "No Nonsense," in our world, they are "Crazy As Hell," but they say that about anybody that ain't having it.

CHAPTER 39

MAY HAVE SAVED MY LIFE

I had so many mixed feeling about Splizzy and how I approach him, how I engage a conversation with him after knowing that he masterminded a kidnapping plot involving my daughter and her mother and had me pay a fake ransom to get my daughter back when there was never a real kidnapping. The whole thing was staged to get me to pay unknowingly, for the murder of my daughter's mother. My daughter would never forgive me if she knew that I paid for her mother's murder. She probably wouldn't care whether I knew or not. If I never told Splizzy to watch her, she'd still be alive because no one would have found out that she was beginning to work with the Feds to set me up. There would still exist the chance that everybody, including her, would have been facing Life or the Death Penalty for killing a police officer.

I considered that Splizzy may have saved my life by taking hers. I also considered whether he would take my life to save his. I needed to see him so I could see the expression on his face when I asked him why he didn't come to me so I could have made that decision. Then and only then would I be able to decide whether he too should die.

It was three hours later on the East Coast which meant that it was 9:00p.m. there because it was 6:00p.m. in California. There was no answer on his cell phone, so I tried the studio and got voice mail before Splizzy called right back.

"Hello," I really didn't know what to say to him without bringing up the situation because that was really all that was on my mind.

"Yo, what's good? I was wondering when you were gonna call. Did China give you my message?" He sounded like he was drunk or high or something because he was slurring.

"What you been drinking, Yo?"

"Yeah, we had a little bubbly with Fabulous and his entourage to celebrate his lil cousin Fresh Kid's album release, but I'm good though. So what's up with you? I thought you would've been called me by now."

"And I thought you would have been come to see me." I sharply shot back.

"Don't start that, you know I hate going inside of prisons. That shit is bad luck. You lucky I came at all to that jail where you was at. The only reason I came down there is because I needed to see you face to face to tell you about Rissa."

There was a momentary silence while my mind raced into deep thought triggered by his mentioning of Rissa's name. What kept running through my mind was why didn't he come to me about Rissa, instead of taking it into his own hands. I still don't know how to take that one.

"I'm not trying to hear that superstitious shit, yo. If you was locked up, I would come holler at you. Hold up......yo, I'll get back at you, somebody is coming, I gotta go."

I ended the call and hid the cell phone inside one of my Timberland boots while the prison guards took forever to count and clear the count.

CHAPTER 40

I'VE BEEN DIAGNOSED WITH...

It had been a long tough road trying to stay out of trouble long enough to make it through the 500 hour drug treatment program and now when I get down to 39 days before release, I get the shock of my life, literally. All I could say is why me? What have I done so bad that I deserved this shit. It just goes to show that money ain't everything. In fact, money ain't shit unless you're gonna be around to enjoy it. I never imagined that I would find myself wondering whether I was gonna die early from A.I.D.S., nor did I believe my ears when I called China to ask her why did she not come to visit two days in a row when she never missed a day. I knew something was wrong then, but never did I imagine for a moment that it would be like this.

She hadn't answered several of my calls nor had she returned any of my messages left on her voice mail. This was not good at all. The phone rang three times before China crushed my world.

"Hello." China answered in what seemed to be a depressed state.

"Dee I'm sorry that I haven't answered your calls. I just didn't know what to say to you or how to tell you what is going on."

"Hold up? Whatever is going on, nothing should keep you away from me but death itself. So unless you are dead or on the operating table getting ready to die, please don't shut me out. We are partners and friends for life. Do you understand that? Plus you holding way too much money to be not answering my calls."

"Dee, I'm sorry, but I've been really depressed and I've been sleeping a lot in hopes that this is all a bad dream...."

I eagerly interrupted, "Hoping that what is all a bad dream? What is going on? What are you talking about? This doesn't have anything to do with that money does it?

"No, this is about me Dee. Better yet, it's about us."

"What about us China?" My patience was running out.

"Look Dee, I still don't know how to tell you this...."

"Just spit it out China, it can't be that bad." I said; not knowing that it could be and was worse than "That Bad."

"I have been diagnosed with H.I.V. and.....I......" she started to break down.

"What? How? When did you hear this?"

"Last Thursday, the doctor called me Dee. I'm so sorry." The silence turned into liquid tears. "Dee, you need to get tested too."

I felt like crying myself. Damn, it took a lifetime to find a true ride-or-die chick, somebody I can trust, somebody that wasn't scandalous or grimy, not to mention was a part of my fantasy of having an erotic ménage trios with two exotic girls. I'll never forget that.

It seemed like whenever I got close to happiness, something always intercepts it before it becomes a reality. Just the thought of China not being around anymore was crazy, but to think that I was also at risk was way too much for me to handle on the way home from prison. And the bad part about it is that the Federal Prison tests you for AIDS upon your request but the results take so damn long that I wouldn't get the results until after I'm released.

This meant that for 39 days, I'd be thinking about and wondering about whether I'm gonna live or die. I knew that shit was too good to be true. I wonder if she had it all the time and either didn't know, didn't care, or she just started caring and her conscience was eating her ass up.

CHAPTER 41

GOOD NEWS

This changes everything. I don't know whether to start making a will and funeral arrangements or whether I can find a cure like Magic Johnson, or whether I might have gave it to Brishette and the baby or Reecee or Candy and the baby. I don't know shit. There's just too much uncertainty right now. If this is a dream, I wish somebody would wake me the fuck up. What bothers me the most is my daughter, what if she has to endure another funeral? Both parents die on her at such an early age. First your mother gets kidnapped and killed, then you find out your father died the same year from A.I.D.S. Damn, that would fuck me up if I were a kid and she's a young girl to make matters worse.

I wasn't writing nobody, calling nobody, and I wasn't doing any visits. I just didn't feel like being bothered. I needed to start moving money around just in case something happens. You just never know what somebody is thinking when they got nothing to live for. I didn't think China would go south on me but people do some strange shit when the doctors tell them they are dying.

After calling Splizzy a few times on his cell and getting no answer, I called the studio. "Hello, Beat Station, may I help you?" This was a sexy voice I never heard before.

"Yeah, can I speak to Splizzy? Tell him it's Dee."

"Please hold...." I hated being on hold. That shit made me feel like I was having an anxiety attack. Everybody used to say I don't have any patience.

"Hello?"

"Damn playboy, what's up? So you got a new receptionist now?"

"Oh, you talking about Malina, yeah I guess you can say she's new. I met her at the Baltimore Arena when Fabulous and them did a show. She was working with catering at the time. She was professional and so beautiful. I offered her a position making more money and she accepted."

"Oh, so you stealing people from the Arena huh, so you ballin like that now?"

"Every since the word got out that Fabulous lil cousin blew up and was all over the radio, shit been taking off. V-103 had me come in and do an interview. Oh yeah, Fabulous was shouting us out on the Michael Baisden Show and now studio time is booked for months."

"Okay baller, so you know I'm home in less than a week right?"

"Come on Dee, you know I wouldn't miss that for the world. I got you homie. Plus, shit starting to look real good on this end. I didn't think the business would take off this fast. I expected at least a couple of years before this happened. I even got a call from Baltimore magazine. Anyway, I'm trying to get everything together so I can be out there when you get out...."

"Hold on somebody's on my other line." I had to be careful answering a cell phone in jail. It could be them people trying to see who answers. "Hello."

"Hey Dee, it's Megan, I've been trying to reach you. I....."

"Yeah, you and a million other people."

"What?"

"Nothing, don't worry about it. What's up Megan? Where you at? Can I call you back cause I got somebody on the other line. No, you know what, hold on...." I clicked over. "Yo Splizz, I'll call you back or call me when you get out here."

"Awight, yo. Peace nigga."

"Megan? You still thetre?"

"Yeah, I'm here. So what's been going on with you Dee? You haven't returned any of my calls."

"Things weren't good for me to be calling nobody, you feel me?"

"Okay, well I have some good news for you. Jay told me to tell you that the boy turned himself in last week to take responsibility for what happened to the F.B.I. agent so that clears his name but he don't know about any other charges. But anything else, we can deal with. It was getting that murder charge out of the way that was the problem."

"That's what's up. Now, that is good news! So, does he know I get out next week?"

"We knew it was real soon. I don't know if he knew it was that soon. So how are you getting home?"

"I don't know yet."

"You want me to come and get you? I can drive up there if you need me to. Plus you owe me something and I want it."

"What are you talking about Megan? What do I owe you?"

"You know what you owe me DeJohn, don't play me like that. You promised me dinner and that we would finish what we started or advance to part two of what we started."

"I'm not messing with you Megan, you'll have me strung out and calling home telling my wife I ain't never coming back like that guy in the Eddie Murphy move, 'Harlem Nights'. " We both broke out in laughter. "I know all about your type, you put a spell on a guy with that good head of yours."

"Whatever; you're crazy DeJohn. You should have been a comedian because you are so funny. No but seriously, let me know if you need me to come and get you, plus you know Jay probably got something planned for you. You already know how he is."

"Yeah, I know. I think I'm good though. I'll let you know if I need you." There was no way that anybody but China was picking me up. I wasn't trying to see nobody until I got with China and secured my money. I don't care if the president wanted to pick me up. "Tell Jay I said congratulations and let him know I will call yaw as soon as I touch down and get settled in. Okay?"

"That's fine. I'll let him know."

"Alright, I'll talk to you later Megan."

CHAPTER 42

I'M GONNA BE HERE FOR YOU

I was released at 8:45a.m. I said my good-byes to all the "Real Dudes" that I built a rapport with. Some I will definitely see again and some I could care less. Some of my homies walked me to the OUT OF BOUNDS point as I headed for the parking lot and just as planned, there she was - still looking good as ever.

China got out of the Bentley Azure as it glistened under the show - casing heat- projecting sun. China was killing them as usual. She wore a bright yellow short shirt with the Gucci emblem and some yellow tight fitting Capri pants and some gold sandals with a yellow flower across the foot and gold straps, criss-crossed up her legs. She had the tortoise DKNY sun glasses setting it off.

I threw my bags in the trunk, hugged China, turned and waved to the inmates who were up on the hill seeing me off. Some of them were surprised that I kept it real because so many dudes go to jail and tell a million fake-assed stories.

In my head, I must have went over a hundred different scenarios about how to open the conversation but none of them would have been perfect. If I started talking about money first, she may feel that I didn't care about her and her situation and that wouldn't be good at all. If I started talking about her condition, she might want to talk about something else. So I just kept it simple because that always works. "Damn China, you wearing the shit out of that Gucci and it don't look like you have a bra on either." I said smiling.

"It's a lace bra."

"So how is my favorite girl?" I reached over and hugged China, whispering in her ear, "Damn you smell good girl. So how are you holding up?"

"I'm good as can be expected under the circumstances."

"Hold up, don't pull off yet." I reached over and hugged her again this time I gave her an extended hug. "China, I need you to know something, no matter what, I'm gonna be here for you. We gone get through this together. Shit, if we have to go to another country to get the best care or a cure, that's what we're gonna do."

"Dee, I am so numb right now. First, let me apologize for not coming to see you or answering your calls, but after doing the math I was really mad with you, well myself for not taking better precautions..."

"Hold up. Why were you mad at me?"

"Why? Because I'm not like a lot of the girls that dance at the club. A lot of them are having sex with those guys for money. I don't get down like that Dee. I told you before I've only been with a handful of guys in my life and I'm proud of that...."

"You still haven't told me why you were mad at me though."

"You didn't let me finish. Look, it's like this Dee, I just got tested five months ago and the results were negative and I haven't been with anybody but you that night in the hotel when you snuck out. So I have to ask you have you been with anybody else?"

"So what are you saying that I gave it to you? Naw, I got tested not even a year ago and my results was negative and I've been locked up so I ain't been with nobody but you."

"Are you sure you ain't sneak out and fuck some other girl?"

"Yo, I swear on my daughter, I ain't fucked nobody since I was locked up but you."

"Not even your wife?"

"Nobody China, and this ain't making no fucking sense. Take me to that planned parenthood spot on Lacienga so I can get tested and find out what's going on."

"I got a better idea, I'm going to take you to the three hour test site on Hawthorne Blvd.. They guarantee your results within three hours." We got into Los Angeles close to lunch time. The traffic was bumper - to - bumper on the 10 freeway. We didn't arrive at the place until 12:45. Sitting in the waiting area of the Hawthorne Medical Center, my mind began to wander, thinking about the fact that H.I.V. has no prejudices. It doesn't care if you're white or black, rich or poor, if it catches you slipping, you're out of here. Just like striking out in a ball game. None of this was making any sense to me. I had been tested 10 months ago when I got into the system and was negative and I had only had sex with China after testing negative. She is now saying that she tested negative five months ago and has only had sex with me. Doing the math would make me the carrier. Naw, fuck that! Ain't no way! At that moment, I had a host of flash backs visualizing all the unprotected sex I had with Reecee, Candy, China, Twyla and my wife Brishette. That could only mean that it didn't show up when I tested ten months ago. I wonder would it have shown up six months later if I had gotten tested again. My thoughts were interrupted by the nurse, "Mr. Patterson you can come on back. Right this way."
China waited in the lobby while the nurse took me back into an exam room and took two tubes of my blood.
"Excuse me Miss, how long does it take to get the results back?" I asked not wanting to be sitting around.
"It takes anywhere from one to three hours."
"The reason I asked is, I wanted to go and grab some lunch and hopefully when I come back yall might have my results."
"That will be fine Mr. Patterson, hopefully we'll have your test results when you return."
China took me to Marie Calenders across from Nordstrom in the Hawthorne Mall. I didn't really have an appetite so I ate a little and picked over the rest. All I could think about was if I am positive, where did I get if from and how do I explain to everybody that I got AIDS and I'm gonna die? I never really looked at life this way before. When something tragic happens, it makes you appreciate the small things in life, like waking up in the morning, being able to walk, having people around you that really care about you and not what you have or what you can do for them.

On the way back to the Medical Center, quietness filled the air as I took in the sights on Hawthorne Boulevard. "China pull over, stop the car! Let me out right here!"

"Why, what's wrong? You gotta throw up?"

"Just pull over China. Right here! Right here!"

I got out of the care in front of this huge cobber stone structure and walked through the huge double-doors. I felt like I was walking the Green Mile as I walked down the dimly-lit isle up to the burgundy carpeted altar and dropped to my knees. Immediately I felt a sense of anxiety and fear confirmed by the butterflies in my stomach.

I didn't know what I could say to or ask of GOD, but I knew I needed God's help to get through these troubling times. Just like the old TLC song goes, "I ain't too proud to beg."

As I contemplated what I could say, I felt China's hand embracing mine with a reassuring squeeze as she also kneeled beside me and whispered the words, "The Lord will help us get through this."

We said our silent prayers which lasted a few minutes, then as we raised up from the altar, China's sniffles-indicating her crying-could be heard throughout the church's quietness. It's funny how when things are going well, people, including myself, always seem to put GOD and prayer on the back burner. Then as soon as something goes wrong, it's "Oh GOD, please help us." It made me think about being a father. I hope my children don't grow up only coming to me when they need something because I'm gonna feel some kinda way about that.

CHAPTER 43

THE MOMENT OF TRUTH

Damn, since the time we left, it seemed like an eternity. I couldn't wait to get this over with but another side of me didn't want to know because if I am positive or "hot" as we called it, then my whole life as I know it today, would be over. I'd be living a different life, a life of constant thoughts of when I'm going to die, thoughts about how will I look when I get real sick, what am I gonna tell my daughter, my sons, my wife, my mother? I wish I knew Magic Johnson, I'd definitely be on the phone with him right now. The nurse saved me from the downward spiraling thoughts that dominated my mind as we awaited my fate in the lonely lobby. "Mr. Patterson, the doctor will see you now. You can come on back."

Already I was not liking the way this was going. I thought I would come in and go up to the counter and say I'm here for my results and they will hand me a piece of paper which says yes or no, positive or negative. I never would have thought I'd be waiting around. Then came the moment of truth. "Mr. Patterson, how are you? My name is Dr. Colliard and I've got your test results here somewhere...." it seemed like he was purposely stalling as he went through the manila file on his desk. "Ah yes, here it is. Well it looks like your results are negative. I'm sure that's the news you were hoping for but as I tell all our patients, you must get tested again in about six months because just because your results are negative this time doesn't always mean it will be negative in six months. Although 8 out of 10 cases will be negative."

Man I wanted to jump up and hug this old white man. "Thank you Doc. I'll just come back in six months for a follow-up test. I appreciate everything."

"Oh, and Mr. Patterson, these are for you. You should keep some on you at all times."

The doctor handed me what looked like a 12 pack of different color Lifestyles Condoms. I smiled, "Oh okay doc, thanks again." I took the cheap condoms and walked out into the hallway where I briefly contemplated how to deliver the good news to China, at least she won't be thinking I gave her the disease.

I could see the anticipation on her face. "So what they say DeJohn?"

"They said I'm negative." I handed her the results so she could see them herself. "Let's get out of here." The look of puzzlement covered China's face as she read the results.

Once we were in the car, China said, "This is crazy," and in my mind I was thinking the same fucking thing.

"What is crazy China?"

"Dee, I swear to you, I have not been with anybody but you and you don't have it then how did this happen? This shit just doesn't make sense."

All that kept going through my mind is she's either lying and covering up her sexual escapades or maybe she got drunk one night and something went down that she doesn't remember. I know she knows that we're just friends so she doesn't have to lie to me. I wanted to tell her to stop fucking lying. You don't just get HIV from breathing air. Then I started thinking about the test results, what if my results were wrong, what if her results were wrong? I began looking out the window, thinking about my wife Brishette and surprising her tonight after I go with China to the mansion and find out what's going on with my money.

I broke the silence. "So how is everything at the new spot? Come to think of it, I never even got to see the inside of the joint."

"Well don't worry about that because we should be there in thirty minutes. Oh yeah, this was gonna be a surprise Dee, but I'm a tell you now...."

"Tell me what now?"

"We got a new spot in San Francisco and guess who's gonna be running it?"

"Who?"

"Your Jamaican cutie."

"Who Twyla? How does she know anything about running something?"

"That girl is very smart Dee. You didn't know but she was here for about three months. I couldn't bring her to visit because she wasn't on the visiting list. Did she ever tell you that her father was one of the original members of the Voodoo Posse of Jamaica and she used to live with him when her mother was in jail for prostitution? She's got quite a past for a young girl, plus she's a fast learner."

"So what other surprises you got for me? You seem to be full of surprises."

"So what's that supposed to mean?" Balling up her face like she had just bit into a lemon.

"Calm down, it's a good thing. Your surprise was a good one."

"Well, the surprises have only just begun, so you might as well brace yourself." China said with a sneaky grin on her face. I know she's not talking about sex because that's kinda the last thing on my mind right now. Don't get me wrong, if there was anybody that I will sympathy fuck while they are HIV positive, it would be China because she was there for me through thick and thin. Just like my wife only my wife don't know everything that's going on in my business life. If I had never met my wife, China probably would have been the one I married and she needs me right now so I am gonna be there for her.

"So what's going on with the money China? I hope you ain't got a bunch of cash laying around."

"Dee just have a little patience. That's part of the surprise. Just chill with me, we're almost there."

I didn't know what to expect but from her eagerness to get me to the mansion, I could tell that she didn't have a bunch of bad news. So I sat back, closed my eyes, and enjoyed the smooth sounds of Sade. I was enjoying that surprise, China remembered that Sade was my favorite and had the Best of Sade playing throughout our ride.

CHAPTER 43

LIFESTYLES OF THE RICH AND FAMOUS

I couldn't believe it. China had exceeded my expectations. I immediately saw the difference in the two mansions. The old one didn't have as much land around it, however this new estate was surrounded by hundreds of acres of land. There was no iron gate but getting onto the property was very tricky because there were so many different roads that led to dead ends. She told me as we seemed to travel a maze to the huge structure.

Damn, this joint looked better than both of the other mansions. China did a better job picking out a mansion than Steph; probably because she wasn't limited to just picking a property who's owner was from out of town. That's the beauty of having cash because cash is king and cash creates convenience.

As we pulled into the huge five car garage, I found myself thinking back to my childhood watching the T.V. series "Lifestyles of the Rich and Famous," with Robin Leech. That show is what probably had me sprung on having a mansion and living the life of a superstar celebrity when I grow up and to realize that dreams do come true makes you wanna pinch yourself.

China walked over to what looked to be an elevator and turned the key. The garage door immediately descended almost as if to signal that the elevator would not open while the garage door is open, a measure of security. I kind of liked that.

We stepped out of the elevator and I knew that a woman was running things because there were plants everywhere in the long hallway. China took me to a room in the middle of the hall. "Dee, I need you to close your eyes."

"Close my eyes? For what China?"

"Just close your eyes, it's a surprise." I closed my eyes and China walked me into the room guiding me to a plush leather love seat in the middle of the room. "You can open your eyes now."

"Oh my GOD girl!" This must have been China's new lavender room. It was crazy. There was a stage with three stripper poles in front of me. On one side of me on a marble table, there was a bottle of Cristal lodged in the sterling silver ice bucket, to my left, there were two Victoria Secret bags filled with something. "China what you got up your sleeve?"

"Nothing right now. This is just the prequel to what's coming. I just bought you here so we could talk briefly and I could show you that your money and anything else that you trust me with is and will always be safe with me."

With that she reached over and grabbed the two black gift - bags from the table and sat them in front of me. The top of each bag was covered with lavender tissue concealing its contents. China pointed to the bags, "Don't you want to know what's in it? Aren't you curious?"

"You're a trip girl." I said as I pulled the tissue paper out of the first bag. There was a gold Presidential Rolex and the lights overhead bouncing off the diamonds liked to temporarily blinded me for a second. Damn, that shit was touching. China was now pouring two flutes of champagne and handing me one.

"Damn China, I appreciate this. All of this is for me?"

"You are the President right? I'm just your CEO and CFO, but you put this together and you changed my life DeJohn. So no matter what happens I'll always remember that you treated me better than family. Now go ahead and finish looking in the bag because you're making me get all emotional and shit over you."

I removed some more of the tissue from the bag and uncovered a fold-up key. "What's this for China?"

"That's the key to your new Range Rover. Your coming home present from me."

Damn, I never expected all of this. I had to express my gratitude. I was really touched by her gesture. "Come here China." I grabbed her hand and sat her down on my lap putting my arms around her and began to kiss her. First her cheek, then her forehead, and finally her tender lips. I had taken the AIDS awareness class at Nellis Air Force Base and I knew my limits, so kissing China was not something that I could contract AIDS from, unless she was bleeding.

China held me so tight. I guess she felt my sincerity as I whispered, "China, I'm with you every step of the way, like Bonnie and Clyde and I mean that from my heart." I squeezed her even tighter to let her know it's all good. China's tears started to roll down her face onto my shoulder.

"Okay DeJohn, let me get myself together. Look, there is two hundred and fifty thousand in the bags. You can go shopping, take your family on a little vacation or something on me. This is not out of your cut. This is my money and I want you to enjoy it. Oh yeah, I almost forgot. One of the VIP guests has a business called MAKE-UPS.COM."

"What is that?" I asked.

"It's a gift and telegram service that you call when you want to do something special for your significant other. It was designed for people who want to make up by blowing their spouses' mind with some unique surprise. Like he explained, they have singers who deliver a telegram in person and give your wife roses and a card from you and it's all video taped so that you'll have that special moment on tape forever, or they can surprise her while you're having dinner with a saxophone or trumpet player, who might blow her favorite tune while she eats or something."

"So why you bring that up, I don't need to make up to nobody. I ain't do nothing to make nobody mad at me."

"I know, I just thought we might use them to surprise your wife tonight. They said they can be ready within an hour and a half to two hours."

"Ohhh, okay, I'm feeling that China, that's a good idea. Let's set that up and you said that they video tape the whole thing right?"

"Yeah, so you need to let me know where they need to go so they can estimate a time."

China got the guy on the phone and had me explain exactly what I wanted done. Two hours later, I sat across the street in my new black Range Rover with the peanut butter leather package and tinted windows, compliments of China, watching the whole thing and just as he finished singing her favorite Luther Vandross song, "House is not a Home," I got out of the truck and walked over there. Her eyes lit up like a kid on Christmas. The video was rolling the whole time.

"Oh my GOD, DeJohn, baby you're home. How...." before she could finish her question, I grabbed her pulling her into my arms and began kissing her with such passion that you would have thought that I hadn't seen her in ten years. To taste her tongue again was like a delicacy. "You're full of surprises. So, how did you pull this off?"

I smiled and stated, "Don't worry about it, I still got moves, where's the baby?"

"The baby is sleep."

I tipped the singer and the video guy each with a crispy fifty dollar bill. They gave me the tape and left.

CHAPTER 44

THE HOT REUNION

Once inside, the fireworks began. It had been what seemed like forever; counting all the time that I couldn't get any while she was pregnant, then on top of that, the year and some change that I was locked up in Federal Prison. That's a long time to be waiting to make love to your wife.

I gently grabbed her arm and spinned her around towards the wall putting her arm on the wall and then the other one. "Against the wall, I need to frisk you. You don't have any drugs or dangerous weapons or anything like that on you, do you?"

"No sir, I don't. What's this all about officer?" Brishette said playing along with my lead. I started with her soft hands slightly brushing down her hands to her wrist then to her forearms. My adrenaline started to flow. I put my left leg between her legs, slightly kicking her left then right leg aside. "Spread 'em."

"Officer can I ask what this is all about?"

"Listen mam, I'm asking the questions here, not you! Do I make myself clear?"

"Yes..." Brishette was wearing a pair of Moschino Jeans and a matching Moschino tee-shirt.

"Why are you breathing so hard mam?" Brishette's breathing had increased as I began to feel on her perky, now hardened nipples. I could tell she wasn't wearing a bra because I felt no straps or fabric beneath the t-shirt. As I gently massaged her breast, I leaned my chest against her back, allowing my now swollen love muscle to rest and perfectly fit between Brishette's perfectly rounded butt. As my hands descended down to her stomach and beyond I asked, "So mam, you wouldn't be hiding anything in your pants would you?" I quickly frisked down her right leg, then down her left, then I made my way back up her legs.

"What about between your legs mam? Are you hiding anything that you wanna tell me about because if I find that you are hiding something, you will be charged with lying to an officer."

I began to grope her three-finger gap, rubbing her plump softness through the jeans. I could almost feel the moistness building inside of her panties.

"Why are you shaking mam? I think you're hiding something and I'm gonna have to perform a cavity search. So I'm gonna need you to take off your clothes mam."

"But sir, I'm not used to taking off my clothes in front of a complete stranger. You could at least call for a female officer to search me." I continued to unfasten her jeans and pulled them down over her hips revealing the golden glow of her skin. Just seeing her flesh sent my blood racing. "Mam, unless you want to be charged with resisting arrest, I suggest that you cooperate and if you're not hiding anything, then it shouldn't be a problem."

As soon as her pants and panties were down just above her knees, I slipped two fingers into her juicy palace. "What are you doing officer?" Brishette panted.

"I'm checking you for contraband mam, just keep you hands above your head mam." I guided both arms closer together and pulled her T-shirt over her head, exposing her entirely naked body down to her knees. I pushed her pants to her ankles and removed one leg at a time. Now completely naked I said, "Mam, I'm going to have to ask you to turn around facing me, with both hands above your head." Brishette turned facing me with that 'Damn, I'm ready' look. I began caressing her breast, "Mam, I'm gonna have to ask you are these yours or are they implants? A lot of women have been known to transport drugs in what is believed to be breast implants. I'm sue you've heard about it on the news mam."

"I assure you officer that these are my own and not implants." Brishette was playing her role all too well. I knew that I would one day test her acting skills and just as I expected, the well respected screen writer acts just as well as she writes. And I see why she was nominated for best screen-writer.

Her breathing intensified as I slowly massaged every inch of her now erect breast. Once she began a low pitched moaning, "Hmmm" I knew it was time. I gently pressed my lips against hers, slipping my tongue deep into the mouth I longed for, for close to a year. I felt the fire ignite between us. Brishette grabbed my sweatshirt from the bottom and began raising it over my head. Then her hand went into my sweatpants groping my swollen "ready to go stick."

Brishette quickly pushed me against the wall and slid down my sweatpants and boxers. We had shoes and clothes scattered about the hallway floor. Just as I stepped out of my last leg, I felt the silky warmth of Brishette's mouth in a slow progressive motion, covering my throbbing member in an attempt to deep throat me. Damn, and just when my mind sent messages to the rest of my body to close my eyes and relax and enjoy this, she abruptly stopped, sprang to her feet and took off running down the hall laughing.

"Oh, hell no." I blurted out before taking off after her. Just as I caught up with her, she stopped in front of the baby's room and put her index finger up to her parted lops signaling to be quiet. She peeped inside the room with me peeping over her shoulder and we saw that the baby was still sleep.

Once inside the bedroom, Brishette stated, "Let me turn up the baby monitor so we can hear if the baby wakes up."

"You just make sure you don't wake up the baby with the screaming you're going to be doing."

"And why would I be doing all this screaming officer? I'm not gonna have to sue you for police brutality am I?" She said with a wicked smile before I pushed her on the king sized bed.

"Mam, because you tried to escape, I'm going to have to teach you a lesson." I grabbed both hands and stretched them out to each side of the bed and began nibbling on the inside of her left arm sliding my tongue down the contours of her arm. I activated the erogenous zone and sent pleasure ripples throughout her body; evidenced by the moaning and squirming she was doing. I repeated the same motion on the other arm then started working on my second favorite zone, cupping and taking her right breast into my mouth, circling my tongue around the nipple. As I equally worked the left breast sending duplicate pleasure signals to the middle to assure her wetness.

I reached down between her legs and began rubbing her moistened clitoris while licking in circles over her stomach region. When I reached her pelvic region, Brishette couldn't keep still. I had found another erogenous spot that stimulates her. I noticed as she squirmed, her legs parted with anticipation of feeling my tongue-magic.

I got in position to deliver a mind-blowing session of cunnilingus, I think that's what they called licking pussy in college. Anyway, I started drawing little zig-zag patterns on her inner thighs, then following up with my artful tongue in a similar pattern, sending racing pleasure signals throughout Brishette's voluptuous body. As she felt my tongue grow closer to her magic pearl, her legs responded with a mind of their own, instinctively parting like the red sea. I spread the lips of her sugar walls and started a wet circular exploration mission with my tongue.

I had her clit right where I wanted it; under submission, between my tongue and the peak of my upper lip. As I commenced the twirling motion, she started that French-styled moaning and that set me off. I stuck my tongue deep inside her wet box, while inserting one finger in the back door.

She grabbed my head with both hands trying to keep me at that one spot until she came. She had to know by now that my objective was to try to make us come together. So I quickly made the transition to sixty-nine position. There's just something that happens to me when I'm getting head, good head. Damn Brishhh, I thought to myself as I tried to send her to the moon by sucking the shit out of her juicy pussy. Brishette had every inch of me inside her mouth. The deep-throat game was in effect. That shit felt so good. The first out-of-jail sexual experience. All of a sudden, she stopped. Of course, I couldn't help but look up and noticed her reaching for something; so I stopped. She came back with some kind of oil. She opened it and put some on my dick, making it instantly warm then icy cool, when she blew on the head . It was some kind of icy-hot oil.

It was obviously flavored because Brishette started licking up and down the shaft and popping the head in and out of her mouth in a teasing fashion. I couldn't take it anymore. I ended the fellatio session and moved between her legs.

I guided my swollen member into her love box and began to deliver long strokes of passion. The kind of passion that I've been longing to give my wife for little over a year.

"Wait DeJohn, ouch. That hurts baby. Take it easy! Remember, I've been keeping it nice and tight just for you...."

We made love for about an hour and a half before taking a shower and falling asleep in each others arms. It felt so right to be in the arms of my beautiful wife and this time I'ma do everything that I can to make sure we're never apart again.

CHAPTER 45

I FELT THE HELICOPTER LANDING

In the middle of the night, I was awakened by the baby monitor. My senses were still on twenty-four hour alert, just like in jail where you had to sleep with one eye open and be ready at all times if something jumped off like a fight, a shake-down, a fire drill, or anything crazy like that. I went in the room and picked up my son, changed his pamper and put him in the bed with me and Brishette.

I woke up to the beautiful smell of home-cooked fried potatoes and onions. The aroma of oven-fresh biscuits being prepared in the oven, coupled with the sound of my little son starting to cry right next to me in a real bed, not some little vinyl mat that we had to sleep on in federal prison.

Damn, even the sounds of my son crying in my ear, was like a dream come true. Being in prison makes you appreciate the small things in life. I felt so good to be home with my Brishette and the baby starting a new life. Looking at my son made me realize how important it is for me to stay out of jail. It seemed like as soon as I picked him up and held him in the air, looking into his eyes, he stopped crying and started smiling. It's like our father-son bond had became official at that moment.

"Hey little-man. You missed your daddy huh?"

Brishette walked in with a sterling silver platter filled with a plate of mouth watering pretty yellow with a little orange-colored cheese melting throughout the eggs. There were several slices of turkey bacon, some fried potatoes and onions that other people called "home-fries" and my favorite piping-hot buttered croissants with orange slices around the plate like a gourmet chief prepared it. Then to wash it down, there was a half of carafe of what looked like fresh squeezed orange juice.

"I'm so hungry, I could eat a horse right now. Here, take the baby so I can brush my teeth and wash my face."

"Come on lil man, let mommy get that baby right." Brishette cooed, making him smile.

I left the room to brush my teeth and get "them men", it's what we called bad breath in prison, out of my mouth and smash my breakfast before it got cold.

After breakfast, Brishette had her sister come and get the baby. And our day began with her taking me to see thee new home that she committed to buying from her doctor friend, who she said was moving out of the country. The house was huge, with four bedrooms, a pool, a big back yard for the kids to play in , a two car garage, and it was nice and secluded, away from it all. But, Palm Springs, was way out of the way. A place far away from ,the hustle and bustle of the Hollywood scene. A place where my family could be safe from the gangs. But I knew I wouldn't feel my family was safe until I had them much farther away from it all.

After we checked out the house, we went shopping at the posh Palm Springs Mall. It felt so good to be back in the real world outside those prison walls. I went crazy buying everything I saw, from silk boxers and wife beaters to Brionni, Canali, and Armani suits. Oh, you know I had to get the I'm Back collection of Faragamo and Cezar Picaulte shoes.

We had a manicure and pedicure together; then did lunch at a restaurant called Sagio's-the great Wolfegang Puck;s exclusive new restaurant. We found a cool barber shop called "Cuts Above The Rest" that gave me the hot-towel and razor treatment. I felt like Don Corleone in the God Father. Just the looks that I got from women as they passed by Brishette and I as we walked to the car, made me know for sure that I was looking as good as I was feeling. Brishette sensed it too because she tightened the grip she had on my hand as if to say to the girls, don't even think about it, as we were approaching the car.

I marveled at the beautiful serene scenery filled with lavish homes and Palm trees that reminded me of what life had in store for me. It was simply priceless. During the trip back, I fell asleep to the sounds of Luther Vandross and Frankie Beverly and Maze. I woke up to Brishette's voice, "DeJohn, wake up! We're home. C'mon we've gotta get dressed for dinner. I'm taking you some place special tonight. It's a surprise."

"What time is it?" I asked, getting myself together unfastening the seat belt to get out of the car.

"It's 7:05 and we've got a reservation for 8:30 so we've gotta hurry and get dressed and get out of here."

I wanted to take a shower with Brishette but she protested because she knew we could wind up making love in the shower. She was right. So I waited until she got out to take my shower. When I got out, Brishette was half-dressed and had laid out my olive-colored Armani single-breasted suit with an ecru-flavored oxford button-down shirt with an earth-tone Gucci tie and brown socks that made the smooth fashion connection with my brown baby-soft Faragamos. I just put the Bulgari watch on, I was still killin em. We were out of the door by 8:10pm, headed to what I thought was a restaurant, but turned out to be the airport. "Why are we at the airport Brishh?" I asked with a look of puzzlement.

"DeJohn, we have to hurry. C'mon, the guy is waiting for us."

"Hold up Brishh, what's going on...?"

"DeJohn, you're holding up progress. Look, the restaurant I'm taking you to is an exclusive restaurant and they have this package that includes a helicopter ride to the restaurant and back. They blindfold you right before you get there...."

"Blindfold you? I never heard of a restaurant like that before."

"DeJohn, you're from the East Coast, you haven't been here long enough. There are a lot of things that you don't know about California. California is full of surprise getaways, just work with me DeJohn."

Once we boarded and the helicopter lifted off, Brishette began grinning this Cheshire cat smile. "What are you smiling so much for? What are you up to Brishh?"

"I'm just happy that you're home and I want to show my husband a good time. Do you have a problem with that?" Brishette reached over and placed a soft sensual kiss on my cheek.

"No, I just wanted to know what you got up your sleeve, that's all." I said smiling. Minutes later, I found myself being blindfolded. I had to remember that my wife is a movie screen-writer, so drama is her middle name. So it would take her to find something like this. I felt the helicopter landing.

CHAPTER 46

LOUIS XIII

"DeJohn, we're here. I'm gonna get out before you so I can help you down, okay?"

"Don't let me fall."

"I won't. C'mon, just watch your step."

Once on the ground, Brishette held my arm tightly as she guided me through the door of the restaurant; but something was up because I didn't hear a bunch of conversations and silverware hitting the plates. Brishette removed the blindfold and there must have been at least 100 people, a lot of whom I didn't know from a can of paint, scream "SURPRISSSSSE!!!"

The first to greet me were China and Splizz. "Welcome home Dee." China yelled over the noise, wrapping her little arms around me to give me a hug.

"So all yaw was in on this huh?"

Splizz responded "Yo, you know we had to do it big for my main man." We shook hands and embraced.

"Damn, who the hell are all of these people man?" I asked smiling and looking around at all the strange faces.

"I don't know who all these mutha fuckers is." Splizzy threw up his hands.

"DeJohn your friends are here from Palm Springs." Brishette stated as if she expected me to know who she was talking about.

"What friends are you...." before I could finish my question, Jay and

Megan came over.

"What's up Dee? Welcome home man. Damn, how long has it been? It seemed like forever, you looking like you've been taking care of yourself."

Megan joined in, "Yeah, you must have been working out in there or something because you look like you've gotten bigger."

"Yeah, I worked out a little bit; but shiiit, you look like you've been working out yourself Jay, unless you just been eating real good round this mutha fucka."

"You know me, it was once said that "life is what life does," you feel me?"

"Yeah, I'm definitely feelin that."

Go ahead and move around man, there's a whole lot of people waiting to see you up in here. We'll talk later, after everything has settled down or we can talk tomorrow. Oh yeah, my brother is around here somewhere. He probably got lost with one of these bad-assed girls you got running around here."

Steph and Lashonda came over and greeted me. "Heyyy, what's up Dee? What's really happening? Look at you, you killin em with that suit partner. You remember my girl Lashonda right?"

"Yeah sure, how are you doing Miss Lashonda?"

"I'm good. Everything is lovely. The question is how are you doing? I know you are glad to be out that awful place and get back to the good life."

"You know that's right baby-girl."

"Okay Dee...." Steph said taking Lashonda by the hand and leading her away. "We're not going to hold you up; we'll talk to you after you do all your greetings. The natives are getting restless...waiting to see you. Oh yeah, I almost forgot... a party ain't a party without the "Loui." Steph handed me the burgundy leather case, carrying the crystal hand crafted $1300 dollar bottle of Louis XIII cognac; the drink of kings.

As I moved through the crowd, I noticed China waving me over. When I approached, I noticed she was talking with the white boy Josh, the millionaire hacker, who had a black guy with him.

"So we meet again." Josh extended his hand. "But on much better terms. This is a nice place you got here. I see you are about your paper; when I grow up I want to be like you." Josh laughed with an approving hand-shake; moving his head from side to side, nodding it up and down.

"How is everything going Josh? I really appreciated all your work and I look forward to working with you in the future."

"Oh, you don't have to worry about that, China seems to have you covered there; but I didn't come here to talk business. We've got plenty of time for that. We'll be meeting soon anyway to discuss our next venture. Let me introduce you to my partner in crime. This is my main man Kyle. They call him Deep. You think I'm a beast, he's the best that I know in this business."

Deep stood about 6ft tall with a mocha brown complexion and broad shoulders. He wore a black leather jacket over a t-shirt and black jeans, typical hacker or geek gear I though. He must be one hell of a dude I said to myself. "That's quite a reputation you've got. It's nice to meet you Deep." I reached out to shake his hand, "I'm sure we'll make a lot of money together." I said shaking his hand while looking him straight in his eyes. The old heads always told me that the window to the soul is the eyes. You look a man in the eyes and you can see if he's a real dude or not. Most times this held true.

"No doubt, my man Josh tells me that you and China here, are the brains of this dream come true. This is actually brilliant, I would have never thought of this in a million years. So Josh also tells me that you guys are trying to take it to the next lever and start taking this thing on the water with exclusive yacht parties." Deep stated with a look of impression, as if he was impressed with the thought of being around brilliant minds like his own.

"Yeah, that's China's dream so we gotta make it happen, you know what I mean?"

China interrupted "Speaking of making it happen, we've got to keep it moving because everybody is trying to see you and we've got a surprise for you. So please excuse us gentlemen, he'll return shortly."

"That's cool, do your thing. We'll be here enjoying the scene." Josh stated with a school-boy grin on his face, almost as if he couldn't contain his crush on China. That made me wonder whether China and Josh may have fucked around while I was locked up. Even though he wasn't her type and she swore that she hadn't been with anyone but me, he and everyone else was on my suspect short list for giving her that shit.

CHAPTER 47

LAVENDER ROOM

As China led me through the crowd of strangers, mostly women, who seemed to either know me or have no idea who I am. I spotted my main man and old head, Mel. "China I just spotted Mel over there by the couch. So you invited everybody hug?"

"Yeah, they just asked about you and I told them that I'd get you for them, but first I have to introduce you to some of the girls, this is Sizzle."

"Hi. How are you doing? Finally, I get to meet you. China talks about you all the time and Splizzy never stops bragging about his homeboy." She said wearing a cool-aid smile that could catch any man's attention.

Damn, she was gorgeous and had a sexy voice. I can see why Splizz was wide open. She was definitely a dime piece. She had long jet-black hair with a golden brown syrup complexion and pearl white teeth. She had high cheekbones, with hazel eyes and long eyelashes. She had to be no more than 5'3 with a small waist and breast, but a big butt to make up for it all.

"Is that right?" I said smiling and cutting my eyes at her. "I've heard quite a bit about you too." I returned.

"I hope it was all good."

"Oh yeah, just that you're good people, that's all. It wasn't nothing bad." I said easing her suspicions. I could also tell that China wasn't feeling all the flirting that was going on, especially now that she had AIDS and she knew I probably wouldn't have done it like that if she was still sexing me, no matter how subtle it was. Next, I greeted Creamy, Silk and Mony before Mel found me being detained by the four sex kittens.

"Youngster, what's going on partner?" Mel shook my hand and hugged me. "Welcome home. You remember our friend the attorney who invited us to his house for the investment seminar?"

"Where's he at?" I asked.

Mel pointed "Over there on the couch with the two girls."

As I looked, he waved. "Oh, so the girls got him under their spell huh?"

That's what it looks like to me youngster, plus he's one of them dirty old men with money youngster." We both laughed at the site of him tricking with the young girls.

China took that as her que, "I hate to break up this reunion guys, but I kept my promise to you and brought him to you and I have to take him to the next event and we're running late. So please excuse us." I felt like a celebrity being ushered to an event by my personal assistant.

China was killin em with a star-studded gold curve fitting Louis Vuitton dress that fell just below her curvaceous hips, accented by the Istanbul pumps.

We made our way through the crowd and disappeared into the quietness of the elevator. I felt like a superstar being led off into a dressing room. The expertly polished brass-like metal doors provided a mirrored image of China and I standing next to each other, shoulder to shoulder. It was the perfect picture to depict our time tested friendship and business partnership. Up to this point, she had never betrayed me and for that, I am eternally grateful. She's earned my trust and respect til the day that one of us dies.

Just as the elevators opened, I thought about my wife and that she had disappeared into the crowd, probably to give me some space. Once again, China escorted me into her favorite Lavender room. There was no question in my mind that China was a Prince fan the way she loved this distinct color of purple.

"Dee I need you to put this on." China handed me a blindfold, as I sank down into the comfortable black leather seat in the middle of the floor.

"What's with all this blindfolding shit?"

"You don't trust me? You know I would never do anything to hurt you Dee. Just trust me on this one okay? I got you."

I did as I was asked and played along with the game. The next thing I heard was the familiar sounds of Jay-Z's "Show me what you got"; the title track from the Kingdom Come CD.

I could hear the sound of several pairs of heels walking in tune with the music, coming closer to me. As the smell of seductive fragrance filled the air, I felt a soft touch caressingly move from the bottom of my neck up the back of my head, removing the blindfold, revealing the three masked dancers wearing nothing but black cat-woman masks and patent leather bikinis with matching go-go boots.

Although I could not recognize any of the masked seducers, I had a feeling that China might be one of the sensuous dancers. Maybe she was the one who poured and handed me a glass of champagne.

Each one of the sexy cat-women returned to the stage and began to perform their very own version of poll-gymnastics. They seemed to be working the three polls as if they were auditioning for dancer of the year.

As the exotic dancers ascended on my position, the Pussy Cat Dolls "Don't you wish your girlfriend was hot like me, don't you wish your girlfriend was a freak like me, don't cha..." blared through the speakers strategically located throughout out the room. The girls danced around me being sure to rub all up against me. I must say, the girls were quite provocative.

Then mysteriously, two of the girls returned to the stage and disappeared through the door from which they entered, leaving the third one purring in my ear and gyrating her hips on my lap as she got into the music as if it was her theme song.

Suddenly, without warning, this masked cat-dancer stood up and leaned forward rubbing her perky partially-covered breast against my face, almost as if to say, here suck em. I was definitely brick hard by now and had a slight buzz from the bubbly, but was forced to make a quick decision when what seemed to be an all-in-one move. She popped and dropped her soft, almost naked ass on my swollen member. Then she slid down in front of me, grabbing my zipper.

"Whoa, hold up baby. What are you doing?"

"Shhhh..." she put her finger up to her lips. "Just relax and enjoy yourself."

"I grabbed her hand stopping her from releasing my love stick. "I appreciated the gesture, but I'm a married man and I don't get down like that." I said to her trying to reason with this determined catwoman and buy time to control myself, especially now that AIDS might be running around the mansion.

It seemed like she either wasn't listening or was determined that she was gonna suck me off because she tried again with the other hand, causing me to grab both of her wrists and push her backwards. She fell on her ass and began grinning.

"Oh, so you like to play rough, huh? I like it rough." She said raising to her knees and crawling back towards me. But now, I was up standing in front of her. "You must think this is a game. I told you I'm married and...."

Before I could finish, she stated, "If I was your wife, you'd let me do you?" Then she removed the mask. "Now can I finish what I started?" I couldn't do nothing but smile. As she took me into her mouth. Covering my manhood with saliva and her silky lip gloss. I couldn't take it anymore, I pulled Brishette to her feet and pulled her towards me and dropped my pants as I sat down pulling her thong to the side and lowering her like a crane operator on to the slippery magic stick. She bounced up and down in a rhythmic motion, locking her arms around my neck. Then started jerking fervidly until the passion exploded inside of her, making her love come down like Evenly Champagne King. Seeing her reach her climatic plateau made me bust off inside her juicy pleasure walls.

We kissed and held each other for a few minutes then shared a special moment in the bathroom wiping each other off with a warm soapy washrag before returning to the party, both elated like high school lovers who just got a quickie under the bleachers between classes.

FRAUD CHRONICLES

PRESENTS

PART III

INTERNET FRAUD/URBAN SCENE

CHAPTER 1

DRAMA IN THE HOUSE

It all happened so fast, we had just made it out by the pool, only to hear the noise of the crowd's ooohs and ahhhs, making everyone turn to look inside. As a crowd of spectators gathered for what we learned was a brawl between Sizzle, the exotic dancer, as they liked to be called, who Splizzy claimed as his girl and the girl they called "wet-wet", the girl that obviously had plans of taking over Sizzle's spot. You never want this kind of behavior displayed at your party and although it was embarrassing, it was also hilarious. Security quickly broke it up but damn, it's always a spectacle to have two women, strippers at that, tearing each others clothes off and pulling tracks out of each others hair.

I knew I needed to talk to Splizzy because he was personally responsible for this scene taking place, but no one could find him. Then someone tapped me on the shoulder. I turned around to find it was Twyla.

"Hey Twyla, how are you?" I was surprised to see her.

"I'm good. Thank you." She responded in her sexy Jamaican accent. Twyla was looking like a million bucks too. She was wearing a black one shoulder out blouse or it could have been a super short dress that clung just above the bottom of her butt. Under the sexy dress-blouse, she was rocking some skin -tight Adore jeans with black rhinestones around the seams of the front pockets and down the seams of the side of each leg.

"I hear you're doing big things in San Francisco. So China really looked out for you, huh? She believes you have a lot of potential. So, you think you can handle all of that responsibility?"

"You'd be surprised at what I can 'andle..." The Jamaicans just refuse to pronounce the 'h' sound and I will never understand it. Everybody on the islands can't have a speech impediment.

Before she could finish her statement, my wife walked up, "Who were the girls that were fighting Dee?" She then noticed that Twyla was standing there. "Oh I'm sorry."

"No, it's okay, I was just leaving."

"Two girls that Splizzy is obviously seeing, which is a serious conflict of interest. Did you ever get to meet Twyla while we were in Jamaica Brishette?" I said trying to ease the instant tension between them.

"I believe you told me you had given her the week off, but the answer is no. I never met her."

"Now is as good a time as any. Twyla, this is my wife Brishette, this is Twyla."

I could tell that Brishh sensed something about Twyla. It was that women's intuition at work again.

They always seemed to feel even the slightest hint of an attraction between another woman and their man.

"How are you doing Twyla? It's nice to meet you. You're a long way from home aren't you? Are you on vacation or something?" Brish subtly and swiftly started her interrogation. Probably curious to know what the hell is this young cute-assed maid from Jamaica doing in L.A. at a surprise birthday party for me, where supposedly only my closest friends were in attendance.

"Actually, I am on sort of a vacation, but not from Jamaica. I live and work in San Francisco now."

"So what do you do in San Francisco?" Brish seemed determined to get the 411 on Twyla.

"I work for the company." Twyla must have assumed that Brishette was a part of the mansion operation.

"And what company is that?" Brishette grilled Twyla but before she could answer, China walked up.

"Hey, there you two are. I just came from up stairs looking for you love birds. So how did you like your surprise Dee?"

"Wait.... are you telling me that you were one of three mystery dancers? You were in on this too?"

China raised her eyebrows as if to say maybe, but Brish gave it away when she started smiling. Twyla excused herself and effortlessly escaped the interrogation.

Remembering that I needed to talk to Splizzy, I asked China, "Have you seen Splizzy?"

"Oh, he left to go take care of something. They should've been back by now."

"Where did he go?"

"I think he said that they were going to stop by the club and get something to smoke."

That uneasy feeling quickly hit me. "What club China? Please tell me it's not the club where Sizzle dances."

"Yeah it is, why?"

"Let me hold your phone, and find Steph for me. Hurry up please."

Brishette started worrying. "Dee what's wrong? I know when something is wrong. What is it? You've got that same look on your face that you had when your daughter was missing."

"Brishette just chill baby, let me find out what's going on."

Splizzy's phone continued to ring, and go to voice mail. I tried several times to no avail. China returned with Steph.

"What's up Dee? What's wrong?" Steph asked with a look of concern. I pulled him to the side and whispered, "Remember you told me that Splizzy met them people at the club where Sizzle works and for him to watch his back?"

"Yeah, didn't you tell him what I said?"

"Naw, I never got a chance. I haven't talked to him really since you told me what happened. I was gonna talk to him tonight. That's what I was looking for him for."

"So you didn't find him. He's in here somewhere. I just seen him, just a little while ago." Steph proclaimed.

"Yeah, so did I, but China said he left with one of the girls to go get some weed and she thinks they went to the club to cop from somebody at the club. He might be walking into a trap and I can't

reach him on his cell."
"Where Sizzle at? She know the number to the club."
"Sizzle was just fighting, she's probably up stairs somewhere."
China located Sizzle and the call was placed to the Pleasure Chest.
The manager of the club said that Splizzy was there, but that he had
left with some of the Spanish guys and that was twenty to thirty
minutes ago.

CHAPTER 2

DON'T DIE ON ME

China came pushing through the crowd, "Excuse me, excuse me." I could tell from the look on her face that she was not happy about something. "Dee, we need to go. Lonia just called, they're at the hospital."

"The hospital?" My adrenaline shot through my veins.

"She said that they tried to kill him. They shot him twice before the police drove by and they ran."

"Did she tell you what hospital?"

"Yes, Milan went to get my truck. So let's go we can all ride in my truck." China responded with a look of caring.

"DeJohn, I have a better idea. Why don't you and Steph take the helicopter ride back to the airport and get my car. That would get you to the hospital faster. I'll meet you there because we paid for the helicopter for four hours, so you might as well use it. The pilot is in here somewhere. I'll ride with the girls and we'll meet you there."

"Yeah, that's a good idea. Plus I can get us to the hospital within ten minutes from the airport."

We found the pilot and took the chopper back to the city limits. When we arrived at the hospital, we ran into Lonia in the emergency room. She told us that she was out in the car waiting. She saw the guys walking out of the club laughing then she was one of them pull out a gun and start shooting Splizzy. She told us that the only reason they stooped and ran was that the police just happened to be riding by and heard the shots. They ran and the police chased them.

The young looking doctor came out of the double-doors that seemed to be the object of all our attention for the entire three hours and fifteen minutes. It seemed like an eternity for the surgery to be completed. The doctor gave us his seemingly repeatedly rehearsed spiel. "The operation was a success. He's definitely a fighter. It's going to take some time to heal, but he was very lucky the first bullets pierced his shoulder but the second was inches from his heart. We'll be watching him closely. He's not out of the woods yet, but we believe he's gonna pull through just fine."

Sizzle looked a mess. Mascara had ran down her cat-fight scratched face, carried by a river of tear drops that she cried for her man. I guess she was the making of a true soldier-girl that would be by his side even if it meant getting into beat-down mode. "Doctor can I see him." She cooed.

"I'm afraid not. He was heavily sedated, so he's resting. Let's give it sometime." The doctor said by disappearing down the well lit hallway.

I often wondered would Brishette take off her heels and beat a chick down if it came down to it. I kinda think she would, especially since she showed her wild side by becoming my mysterious catwoman-masked birthday stripper, complete with the emotionally driven sexual favors. I'll be thinking about that for a long time to come. She definitely gets most valuable wifee (MVW) award.

On another note, the crazy reality of this whole seemingly unnecessary situation of the murder of a police officer, my daughter's mother Rissa, and now an attempt on Splizzy's life, was mind-blowing. All this because Splizzy wanted to protect his best friend, me!

Damn, when you look at the whole picture, you see dedication and loyalty in a friendship. The kind you take a life and give your life for. I never got to talk to him about why he did what he did. Well more so why didn't he come to me first and talk to me. The thought of killing him or thanking him still remained a question to be answered.

It had been three days. Splizzy's condition took a chilling turn for the worst. He had slipped into a coma. China and Sizzle were a wreck. She was camped out each time I stopped by to check on him.

CHAPTER 3

SUBJECT: THE NEXT PROJECT.

Today we met the formidable two-man hacker team, comprised of Josh and Deep, joined by the illustrious China and myself.
 Damn my life had changed forever. I'd never be the same again. My Baltimore, but international ways followed me wherever I went. My yearning appetite for success that drew me into risk and danger was alive and relentless. It exceeded it's lifespan almost like a vampire. No matter how many times jail tried to kill it, it seemed to outwit rehabilitation only to become stronger and more demanding. I had to have it the art of the thrill. The mansion parties became a fleeting conquered project. Too safe perhaps. I enjoyed living on the edge more, I needed to have my hands in more mischievousness, but safe was good for family. Being miserable was not good for anyone.
 It was just 2:05pm, the sun was at the height of its daily summer routine. The breeze of an uncertain storm front mixed with the mist of the nearby Pacific Ocean offered some solace, as we sat poolside under the white cabana being served iced tea and Miami-styled tropical drinks by Olivia and Sasha. China's newest addition to the mansion family. Their sunbathed bodies slightly adorned with breathtaking bikinis provided temporary eye-candy for Josh, Deep and even myself.
 The sound of the words Western Union again coming, not this time from Josh, but from his mentor Deep, caused a little concern until Deep offered some relief by adding that there was a easier more sophisticated way of stinging, he called it, Western Union.
 "You guys were very lucky to have pulled off that job with so many

variables. In my opinion, it was too risky. I told Josh this but what's done is done, that's water under the bridge."

"So, what is the easier way?" I inquired looking at Deep but noticing Josh's obvious crush on China as he kept licking his lips then looking over at China. "And how do we fit in?"

"Josh tells me that you've got some attorney friends who set up and handle offshore accounts."

"And?"

"And that's kind of all we're missing except for a few crews to open bank accounts and do pick-ups."

China weighed in, "I don't get it, what's the difference in what Josh did and what you're gonna do? Quizzing Deep.

Deep took a sip of his iced tea and broke it down in laymans terms. "Look, first of all there were too many people involved and where there are too many players, there are too many ways that things could go wrong. The easier more lucrative way is to hack into the Western Union mainframe, get through their firewalls, which is gonna be a bitch, but it can definitely be done. Once inside, I get the list of electronic footprint or E.I.D. (electronic I.D.) for all of the Mom and Pops, the pharmacies, and any other authorized Western Union agents. Western Union has approximately 10,000 agents processing wire services. These Mom and Pops are the key to the mainframe. Why go to the vault with all of its security measures, when the money that's in transit from the Mom and Pops are left wide open. It's like stealing candy from a baby, simple electrical override and a remote access set-up can hijack their terminals.

"Hold up, you're confusing me. Do you mean an electrical surge override?" Josh came to the rescue.

"Yeah, and some simple computer code."

"Isn't that something like what some hackers down in Florida did with the department stores when they scammed forty five million credit card numbers?" China was sounding sharp. I just kept my mouth shut and let her do her thing because I didn't know the lingo like she did.

"Well not exactly. That crew used the R.F.I.D.(radio frequency identification device) loophole to gain access. We will be doing a brute force attack on their system, implanting our botnet Trojans to override their transaction terminals."

I was really lost at this point so I asked Deep to "break it down in street terms so I could understand."

"It's simple. It's like this, I write the code to compromise their firewalls, the botnet does the leg work. Let that little fucker do it's thing all the way up to the mainframe. Once it reaches it's destination, we'll have access to possibly hundreds, if not thousands of Mom and Pops around the country. Do the math 100 times 10,000 is one million."

I interrupted, "So how many people do we need to do the pick-ups?"

"You see, that's the beauty of this method we're exploiting Quick Collect and Swift Pay, which automatically gets the money deposited into business accounts."

"So we have to set up accounts, or you do that too?"

"China already chose some of your girls to open the offshore business accounts using new ID's and those lawyers that we talked about earlier and her Chinese connections. So we should be good to go once everything comes together."

"I'll get in touch with the lawyers and get them on board. That's not a problem." I stated thinking about Mel's east coast attorney friends and whether they would tell him details of what we need them to do.

CHAPTER 4

FIGHTING TO STAY ALIVE

The call came with its perfect timing, just as we were ending the meeting. China's soft pink Motorola flip phone came alive with it's distinctive ring. It was Sizzle with the news that Splizzy had awakened from his comatose state that held him captive away from the harsh reality that he might not walk again. The doctor had told Sizzle that Splizzy took a bullet in the chest that missed his heart by inches and was now lodged in his spine and has found a home there. The wrong move could cause permanent paralysis. This caused the doctors to house Splizzy in a temporary body cast to restrict his movements. It was too risky to try to remove the projectile.

It was crazy seeing my best friend lying there covered in plaster, eyes wandering, helpless, but it beat the hell out of seeing him in a casket. Was it karma? Was it the old adage, 'live by the sword, die by the sword.' He must have died a thousand little deaths while in that operating room. Even in a semi conscious state, the mind has a way of talking, communicating and connecting with your conscious, conveying some deep shit like: man we died and came back, and we dying again, but we got a few left in us, so just stay still under that surgical blade.

Splizzy grunted as I moved closer to the bed. China was right by my side. "We came right away, as soon as we got the call." I said as he reached out for my hand, managing a smile amidst his white body armor.

"What's up Dee?" He managed through his cotton-mouth.

I laughed handing him water. "The question is not what's up with me, but what's up with you cowboy?" The small bit of humor brought a smile to everyone's face, including Splizzy. "so what does the other guy look like?" This was our inside joke. As we were growing up, we used to always get in fights and we made a pact that if we got busted up, the other guy had better be busted up two times as bad or the crew would put it on you some more.

"You know what I'm really mad about?"

"Naw, what are you mad about?" I asked.

"All of this and I still didn't get my weed."

"Boy you are crazy. Maybe that's a sign to leave the weed alone." China stated shaking her head back and forth.

"I could never do that." Splizzy said smiling with the pure look of conviction as if he had sold his soul to 'trees'.

"The guys who did this to you, you know who they are right?" Sizzle quickly aided her man. "I know exactly who they are and I think I know where they hand out too, or if I don't, I can surely find out by just asking about weed."

Here I go again. I just got out of federal prison on supervised release and it looks like either I have to put on my gorilla suit or contract the work out to somebody else to keep from getting implicated in the 'get back' plot. Somebody has to pay for what happened to Splizzy, but what's really funny is how all of a sudden, I don't even want to bring up the situation with Rissa. One reason is that I feel bad that I could have warned Splizzy not to go down there and this wouldn't have happened, but I never got a chance to talk to him because everything went so fast. As soon as I walked into the surprise coming home party. Everybody rushed me, then China took me upstairs for the ultimate surprise where my wife had her stripping debut. I wonder what else she can do that I don't know about. I guess that's another thing about her that I loved, is her being so mysterious and full of surprises. One thing for certain, I'll never forget that night the surprise, the stripping, the sex, or the shooting.

Splizzy started coughing really bad, so bad that Sizzle ran and got the nurse. He was having serious complications. Still fighting to stay alive. The doctors rushed in and told us we had to go. That really made me fell worse because he could still die and I had a chance to warn him but didn't think about it when I first saw him at the party. If he dies, who's gonna have my back like he has for all these years?

His loyalty was unmatched so far except for China, who is like a female version of Splizzy, now with her being H.I.V. positive, death was sure to take her sooner that later. It sometimes takes a lifetime to find loyalty, so the loss of Splizzy and China would be a devastating blow to my empire and my sanity. I guess the saying 'easy come, easy go' holds true to more than money.

CHAPTER 5

MS. CLEO

My phone came alive rescuing me from my temporary state of chaotic uncertain'ty. It was my mother's number.

"Hello."

"DeJohn, what are you doing about this girl of yours? And why haven't you told her that you were home?"

"Ma, I wanted to surprise Isha by telling her Brishette is bringing her out here to keep her company until I get home. But we're gonna surprise both her and DJ, by taking them to Disney World. I always wanted to take them, but never got a chance...."

"Oh, you had the chance alright, you were just running the street chasing those no good girls around. I told you time and time again, that you need to find you somebody nice and settle down because ain't nothing but trouble out in these streets and another thing, you keep running around here with all these girls with no protection, you gonna catch something you can't get rid of."

My mother had a way of predicting the future like Mrs. Cleo,or so it seemed, because it seemed like every time she said something it happened. She used to always tell me that she didn't like somebody I hung out with and that they were bad news, and sure enough, I'd wind up getting locked up with that person and she'd be saying "I told you so." If I had paid attention to her words I would have turned out totally different, but it is what it is and you are nothing today but a sum total of all your yesterdays. Plus I can't be mad because no matter what people say, I think she did a good job raising me as a single parent. All I know is that I loved my mother to death, even thought she will tell on me in a minute if I got a girlfriend and she see me with another girl.

"Awright ma, you right, where is Isha ma?"

"She's around here somewhere. Probably outside with Kiki and the girls from across the street."

"I gotta get ready to go, but I'ma send you some money so you can go shopping and maybe you can take her with you and get her some clothes to wear out here, but I'ma call you back Ma and let you know how I'm sending the money. And please don't tell her about the surprise cause you famous for letting the cat out of the bag."

"I ain't gonna say nothing. Okay DeJohn, I gotta get my other line."

"Awight ma, love you."

"Love you too baby."

CHAPTER 6

WAIT UNTIL YOU GET WELL

It seemed like as soon as I hung up the phone with my mother
Brishetted called.
I answered on the second ring. "Hello."
"Hey honey. What are you doing? You wanna have dinner with me
some place quiet and romantic?"
"I'm at the hospital seeing Splizzy. Me and China."
"How is he doing?"
"Not good. The doctors just put us out because he started having
complications. They said he was doing good at first, but said that he
wasn't out of the woods. Now they don't know if he's gonna make it."
"Wow, I'm sorry to hear that. So are you gonna stay awhile or are you
coming home soon?"
"Hold on Brishh, the doctor just said something to China and Sizzle.
What did he say China?"
"He said that they thought he was having complications from the
surgery but it was just some saliva that went down the wrong pipe.
He said that he's gonna be fine. He's asking to speak to you Dee."
"Oh, so we can go in there?"
"Yeah, I guess so."
Sizzle led the way. When we got inside the nurse was just pulling the
covers up on Splizzy.

"I was hoping you didn't leave me just because I was coughing. You
gotta know I'm not checking out that easy. I couldn't tell you that it
was just my spit going down the wrong pipe because I was choking at
the time. You scared me when you panicked and all these doctors and

nurses came running in here. At least I know if anything ever happens to me and Sizzle can't handle it, she's gonna get some help. That's whats up baby girl. Come here."

Splizzy began kissing Sizzle. "So what happened to your face?"

"You don't wanna know."

"Yes I do wanna know. What happened?"

"Your little girlfriend got out of line and I had to give her a Detroit-styled beat-down."

Splizzy smiled. "Oh yeah, that's right you are from the windy city."

"That's Chicago Splizz." I interrupted.

"My bad. Damn, I get Detroit and Chicago mixed up sometimes. So what happened?"

"Don't go there. You know damned well what happened. You just wait until you get well. I'm gonna kick your ass."

"Will yaw stop the violence." China said laughing.

"I don't know what you're talking about. Whatever it is, I'm innocent. But on a serious note, I need you and China to go to the cafeteria or something so me and Dee can talk."

"Yeah, whatever Mr. Innocent. C'mon China. I know when we're not welcome." Sizzle said rolling her eyes and smiling. "Dee you better talk to him. Get his head right."

CHAPTER 7

GET OUR TARGETS

"Yo, you know I can't let this go right? Them whore-assed dudes tried to take my lights out yo."
"Yo, you just get well. Let me handle them dudes. Plus your cousin Man-Man is on his way out here to put in some work on these punks."
"When you talk to Man-Man?"
"I just talked to him a little while ago. I told' em bring his team. I'll take care of everything. They'll be out here tomorrow. I'll bring him to see you, awright?"
"Yo, I appreciate you coming to see me. Sizzle told me you was here almost everyday while I was in the coma and so how do you plan to get to them boys?"
"I got this. Sizzle said she know where these dudes be at, plus Steph's nephew or brother in-law is in the gang with them and he wants out. We can use that to our advantage. We gone save the brother in-law and get our targets at the same time."
"Yeah, that shit sounds good, but you gotta be on your A-game with these sneaky mother fuckers. I know how they move, but if you get the young boy to give em up, they are as good as dead. Plus...."
"Look, the way I see it, it's simple. Steph's little nephew or brother in-law, whatever the fuck he is, is getting treated like a bitch by the other guys. He said he feels like an outcast and he's sick of it. Or that's what Steph said. That tells me that he'll do anything to get back at them. But when Steph said they raped a girl that he brought over the house, I knew we had an in."
He said when he finished having sex with the girl and went to the bathroom, they went in the room, three of them and raped the girl

and made him watch. Telling him he was either down with the homies or down with the girl and they made him choose. He said the girl kept calling for him to help her and he couldn't do anything. He told Steph he really liked the girl but after that, she won't even speak to him and she's scared to tell because they might kill her."

" I wanna kill them bitch-assed niggaz myself."

"Yeah, that was some cruddy shit they did, but they're gonna get theirs. I promise you that. If this boy, Steph's brother in-law comes through for us, this thing will be all behind us real soon. Then we might have another problem."

"What's that?" Splizzy responded.

"If this boy will give up his people, his homies, then what do you think he'll do if he gets in a jam with the law? We might have to take him out too."

Sizzle and China walked into the room silencing our murder plot.

"You better be finished talking because the hospital is about to kick us out because visiting hours are almost over and I'm hungry for some real food. That garbage they had in the machines was not getting it. I need some real food. Some KFC spicy fried chicken breast with the biscuits still warm out the oven."

"Hold up baby. You making me hungry and you know this hospital don't serve nothing with soul in it or on the front of it."

Just as Splizzy said his last words, the announcement came over the speaker. "Visiting hours are now over."

As we left the hospital, China asked was I going to the mansion or was I going home? The answer was obvious. "China you know that I would love to go back to the spot with you, but my wife just called worrying about me, so I'm gonna go home. I'll see you tomorrow."

"Yeah, we gotta talk tomorrow because I think I know what's going through you mind and I hope you're not thinking about what I think you're thinking."

Sizzle got in and started the car while China and I concluded.

"What are you talking about China?"

"We'll talk tomorrow Dee. Go get some rest. Just remember that I don't know how long I'll be here. So you can't go back to jail. You got two mansion to take care of now.

CHAPTER 8

G.R.S. GRAND RETURN SEXATHON

I wondered what China was thinking about these days, knowing that her time on earth was limited. I sure wouldn't be in good spirits. Then again, maybe I'd be living life like tomorrow was my last day. I went in the house expecting Brishette to be sleep and to the surprise of my life when I saw all the candles and rose petals leading to the bedroom.

The baby was over her sister's house, leaving us to enjoy the night without even the thought of stopping or having to be quiet so as to not wake up the baby. I knew tonight was gonna be my G.R.S.-grand return sexathon.

As I walked down the hall following the rose petal trail, I could hear the soft seductive sounds of Jill Scott, "Show me, show me, show me, show me....showwwwwwwwww meeeeeee. If I asked you to.... Would you doo itttt..." I reached the bedroom door's entrance and saw Brishette laying there on a bed or rose petals wearing a Baby Phat sky-blue sheer teddy with a matching crotch less panty showcasing her completely shaven mound. The lights were dimmed and I heard a background sound of moaning only to find that on the big screen was a porno flick, which showed a woman pleasuring herself with a dildo. Then I noticed the brown rubber look-a-like dick on the nightstand. "I've been waiting for you lover."

"Oh yeah. It looks like you've been enjoying yourself without me."
"Correction, just getting ready for you baby." Damn, the way she said that, accented with a hint of Paris and the seductive look on her face had me tansfixed on the thought of her Parisian pussy. It didn't take me two minutes and I was butt-naked. Manhood standing at attention and ready to deliver passion flavored satisfaction.
Brishette had cleared everything form the nightstand where the Bose radio and clock used to be. Now there was a brown leather tote bag. Almost like a men's shaving bag. Only I learned that there were no shaving products inside. As I was finger-ushered to the head of the bed, Brishette reached out cupping my ass, pulling me forward taking my length into her warm juicy mouth. With one hand, I gently held her head as she slowly teased the head with her tongue with a precision I'd never seen. Maybe the porno movies were teaching her the tricks of the trade, but whatever it was, her skills were getting better each time. With the other hand, I braced myself against the wall. This gave me a direct view of some of the bag's contents at least those that could be seen on top of others.
The moaning and her occasionally looking up at me was really turning me on and although I wanted to cum, I wanted more to please my seductress first. I reluctantly pulled back releasing myself from a little bit of heaven. Only instead of me being jealous or mad that she was pleasing herself with a man-made dick, that may have even been bigger than mine, I decided to double her pleasure. I had seen plenty of porno movies where two men occupied both holes and it looked like the girl was enjoying having two dicks inside of her. So I decided to use her toy to take her to another level.
First I reached into her bag of tricks and pulled out some KY jelly. What the fuck is she doing with KY jelly? I thought as I squeezed some onto my finger.
"What are you doing DeJohn?"
"I'm getting ready to take you to another planet." I then pushed both legs in the air towards her shoulders. Brishette held her legs and was now in 'the buck' position exposing both her front and back doors. Then I rubbed the KY jelly over the opening of her butt hole, inserting my baby finer of my right hand to make certain the lubrication got inside. I used my left hand to rub and guide my swollen love stick

across her erect clitoris, then I slid inside of her. I then removed my pinkie finer and began easing the head of the brown rubber-dick into her anal cavity.

The look said it all. Just when she started moaning with ecstasy, I pulled out, still working the rubber look-a-like in small doses, in and partially out of her ass. I reached into the bag and grabbed her 'pink kitty pleaser' vibrator turned it on with the flick of my thumb, and it roared to life vibrating in my hand. I noticed Brishette's eyebrow raise with curiosity, as if to say, what the hell are you doing with my toys?, but she held her peace. I then lowered the buzzing wand, placing it at the opening of her vaginal lips while I ran my tongue over her moist and swollen clitoris, then I slipped my tongue into her love hole. Brishette started grabbing my head by my ears holding me in position while she gyrated her hips to meet each intense rippling-effect of the three way pleasure principle. First the vibrator sat just above my tongue on her little pearl, while my tongue savored her juices that had started coming down like a busted water pipe, and at the same time, I managed to insert the rubber look-a-like about one third of the way inside her anal cavity. Brishette was shaking uncontrollably. Her hands had locked on my head like vice grips. I then slipped my tongue out and ran it down towards her back door, then up to her clitoris to take over her pearly domain, pushing the vibrator aside sucking on the sensitive clit ever so slightly.

"Oh, shitttt. DeJohhhhhn. I'mmmm cummmmmmmminnnnnggg. Ohhhh my Gohhhhhd babeee!!!!!" I was oozing pre-cum just from hearing my beautiful lover reach a world filled with pleasure. I quickly removed the rubber dick from her back door, putting it on the nightstand. I then guided my magic stick insider of her juicy hole and began banging away in hopes of reaching the ultimate goal of cumming together and although Brishette had already began a series of intense convulsion-like multiple orgasms, it did not take me long at all to bust off inside of her. We both held each other as we came together then collapsed from exhaustion. "That was the best sex ever DeJohn. You're not trying to kill me are you?"

We were both out of breath but managed to laugh. We fell asleep cuddled after pulling the sheet over our soaked-and - wet bodies. Once we woke up at 3:07am, we changed the sheets, took a shower and enjoyed the warmth of each other's body.

ABOUT THE AUTHOR

Bio

Darren Keys was born in Baltimore, Maryland and attended the Morgan State University and Sojourner-Douglas College), where he earned his degree in micro Computers and Business Administration. In 1989, he moved to Los Angeles to pursue a career in acting. After landing a spot in the Berkley Repertory Theater, Darren Keys' artistic talents surfaced, inspiring him to become an actor and writer. Yet Darren quickly found out that writing was his passion. From creative writing classes to avidly consuming the works of his favorite authors, Darren Keys began to shape a writing career of his own. Having written several scripts for stage plays in school, he started writing poetry and short stories. Darren Keys' novels have placed him on the map as one of the best writers of contemporary white collar fiction. Darren Keys' book signing tours with White Powder to White Collar helped propel his novels to #1 on the "White Collar Bestsellers List." White Powder to White Collar was named "White Collar Book of the Year" in 2013. In June 2014, Darren Keys celebrated the Japanese publication of White Powder to White Collar by embarking on a book tour to Japan. Soon after, White Powder to White Collar became a bestseller in Japan. Darren Keys is currently working on part 5 to this sizzling 7-part series and preparing for tour with his new stage play WHITE POWDER TO WHITE COLLAR and working on the new Sizzling TV Series called FRAUD CHRONICLES and the upcoming movie WHITE POWDER TO WHITE COLLAR.

DARREN KEYS

FRAUD MASTERS

Look for our new book trailers, stage plays, and the movies coming soon.

Contact us at fraudchronicles@gmail.com, darrenkeys.com, also like and follow us on facebook, instagram and twitter.

www.ingramcontent.com/pod-product-compliance
Lightning Source LLC
Chambersburg PA
CBHW051827090426
42736CB00011B/1684